Harmfully
Involved

Harmfully Involved

William O. Manning & Jean Vinton

Hazelden
Educational Services

First published, October, 1978
Revised October, 1981

Library of Congress Catalog Card Number: 78-060062
ISBN: 0-89486-056-9

Printed in the United States of America

Contents

Preface

Chemical dependency — the addiction of human beings to mood-altering drugs — has been a serious societal problem as far back in human history as we have any record. In recent years the abuse of so-called exotic drugs has captured the public's attention. Less dramatic but more far-reaching is that for Americans, 90% of our drug problem is the abuse of a single easily obtained and socially accepted drug — ethyl alcohol. Only recently, however, have we begun to explore the ramifications of the addiction which has now been recognized as a disease. Within the past decade, businessmen have begun seriously to refer to alcoholism as "American industry's billion dollar hang-over." And schools are becoming more and more aware of the crippling effects of addiction on both students and faculty.

For years we looked at the term "chemical dependency" as describing the state of an individual who was downtrodden, destitute, and who drank wine from a bottle in a brown paper bag. This, of course, is not the description of most people who are dependent upon alcohol. There is no clear answer to the problem, "Am I or am I not dependent?" Where, when, how does one become dependent? Where, when, how does one leave the appropriate use of chemicals and begin inappropriate use?

It is also very difficult for high schools to answer the question, "Is my youngster dependent?" We know that the progress of complete physiological and psychological dependency usually takes a long time, although psychological dependence can come much earlier than physiological. The question then that must be answered in high schools is, "Is it *possible* for a fifteen-year-old to be chemically dependent?" The only serious answer, of course, is yes.

However, in working with high school youngsters we certainly do not want to be in a position in which a yes or no answer is absolutely necessary before we can begin to help students. An important fact in dealing with youngsters is to realize that most youngsters do experiment. Almost all people exist somewhere on a line from experimentation through use, through misuse, to abuse, and eventually to chronic abuse.

Experimentation	Use	Misuse	Abuse	Chronic Abuse

When youngsters begin to experiment and learn the effects of drugs and alcohol, some ultimately begin to seek those effects. From the stage of seeking effects, one out of seven will go on to dependency. To diagnose and decide whether a youngster has entered the dependency stage is very difficult, so we do not attempt to answer the question, "Is he or is he not chemically dependent?"

Rather, we interject the questions, "Is this person suffering pain? Is this person harmfully involved?"

Harmfully involved means that for a person involved in use, harm or pain results. We feel that anytime a student suffers from use, that student is harmfully involved. We encourage that student to evaluate his use, to take a serious look at it and at the pain which results from it.

The same idea holds true for the adult world. Appropriate use among adults occurs daily. But, in many instances, a person whom we know and to whom we are very close is dependent, yet we do not recognize signs. When signs do begin to appear, concerned persons must decide where on the addiction line an individual is. When pain is present, harmful involvement begins to be treatable. The term "harmful involvement" is interpreted less rigidly than are the terms "chemically dependent" or "drunk." Being classified as "harmfully involved" allows people to take a look at their use and to make appropriate changes. "Harmful involvement" provides less stigma for the individual than harsher classifications such as addict, drunk, or junkie. Using the term "harmful involvement" sets an appropriate atmosphere for beginning recovery from the problem.

There is no shortage of literature on the general subjects of chemical dependency and chemical dependency programs. We have not yet seen, however, a written piece of easily understandable prose which describes in detail the rationale for and the design and implementation of a chemical dependency program in a public school district. The need for such a document obviously exists, if requests for information about the Wayzata continuing school program are a valid indication.

We have purposely taken a nuts-and-bolts approach in

writing this volume in the sincere hope that it may serve as a guide for school administrators, teachers, counselors, and parents who believe that the need for a well-defined chemical dependency program exists in their own school districts. We have not glossed over the frustrations, difficulties, and heartbreaks which were a part of the genesis of the Wayzata Public School Chemical Dependency Program. To have done so would have been an injustice, we believe, to those who are just now beginning to perceive the need for early intervention by trained, caring counselors within the public school systems.

The involvement of school administration in the personal lives and problems of students is a highly controversial issue. While this involvement is not recommended for the faint of heart, it can be done successfully. Although we believe that we are just beginning to scratch the surface of the problems in our Wayzata School District Chemical Dependency Program, we have already experienced enough success to have made the entire effort more than worthwhile. The purpose of a school must be to assist students in making a satisfactory progress through the formal educational world. It is difficult to conceive of a situation in which a student who is chemically dependent can make satisfactory progress. A community with genuine concern for its young people and, indeed, for its own health can come to understand that many signs of unsatisfactory school performance are symptoms of a disease for which involvement in personal affairs may be a necessary step toward recovery. It is for that caring community that this book is written.

Acknowledgements

Whenever someone who is not a professional writer undertakes a project of this sort, that person neither knows nor understands the complexities of writing a book.

To my co-author, Jean Vinton, I wish to give my special thanks, not only for her willingness to work on the mechanics of the book in writing and rewriting, but for her willingness to learn about and become involved in the Wayzata Chemical Dependency Program.

To Don Anderson for his personal dedication as a member of the group who started the program;

To the other chemical dependency counselors and guidance counselors who have given so much to the growth of this program;

To the staff members who have dared to become involved in the program;

To the administration and Board of Education for their support;

To Jim and Lee for their support and leadership with the parents group;

Most of all, to those faculty, those parents, and those students who have found new highs and new ways of getting there, new freedoms in sobriety, and the courage to be role models for the rest of us, I give my thanks and appreciation.

—W.O.M.

Chapter One

"Why Is There a Need?"*

He was only seventeen. Seventeen is supposed to be a carefree time, isn't it? Aren't kids like him supposed to care about football games and parties, cars and girls, and have some kind of dreams about the future? But Wes's dreams rapidly faded as Dr. Manning explained the obstacles that lay between him and graduation. His parents stirred uneasily as the problems were tallied — excessive absenteeism, unfinished assignments, failed tests. It appeared that nothing was o.k. Wes was miserable, his mother clearly on the edge of tears. His Dad, Wes knew, was frantically searching for someone else to blame.

The list of failures ended, just where Wes had known it would — two credits short of graduation with his grade and with a lot of doubt about a couple of other classes. And the principal's last question put a lot of responsibility on him.

---

*For another discussion on this topic and for examples of policies presently working in other school districts, see *The Student Assistance Program: How It Works,* by Tom Griffin and Roger Svendsen, published by Hazelden.

"What are you going to do about it?"

He knew they were waiting for him to say something. The silence was intolerable. But Wes had to sort out his thoughts. Things really were bad. He'd been losing out on a lot lately and it was getting harder and harder to feel good about anything. The guys said Dr. Manning really wasn't so bad. Maybe somebody could help.

"Mom," he said, "I've been getting high quite a lot lately."

"Never mind, Son," she said. "We won't bother Dr. Manning with that. We'll talk about that when we get home. It's a personal family problem."

The silence didn't get any easier. It took Dad a minute to react, but when he did, Wes's hopes for help dwindled.

For a few minutes the talk focused on those two missing credits. Night school would take care of one, and maybe the University had a correspondence course Wes could work on. But that was just talk. Wes knew he'd never make it. They hadn't even heard him. His disappointment was so strong that he almost didn't hear when Manning turned to his mother and said, "Do you drink?"

But Dad had heard. He was on his feet and waving his fist, just like he always did when he got mad.

"God damn it! You keep your nose out of my family's business. You've got no right . . . . "

Somehow Manning got him quieted down. Wes was so numb with nervousness and fear and disappointment that he didn't understand how that happened, but when he started to pay attention again, the three of them were talking about graduation as if nothing had been said. For God's sake, Wes thought. They must know there's something more important than that. He was scared that they'd really never hear him. Dad was talking about how they'd just straighten this whole matter out and get Wes up there with his class. Dad had big ideas about what Wes was going to do next year.

Suddenly relief and horror collided together in Wes's head. Manning wasn't going to let go. He'd said something more about drugs and Dad was up there like a flash, waving his fist and yelling again.

"God damn it! I'll get you if you don't shut up! I'm going to call the superintendent right now!"

Then, out of all that noise, Wes heard Manning asking him, "Wes, do your folks drink?"

Wes knew then what people meant when they said they were so scared they just froze. It was as if a projector had stopped for a minute and the film had stopped running. Nobody said anything. Nobody even moved. But then Dad sat down heavily and said — angry, but kind of dull, too —

"You'd drink, too, if you had to live with a cold sexless bitch like I do."

For the first time Mom had something to say.

"Who wouldn't be a cold sexless bitch, living with a puking drunkard like I do!"

Wes wasn't frozen anymore. He was crying. But so was Mom. And Dad.

Well, anyway, it was finally all out in the open. Maybe now something would change.

For a long time, an interview such as this would have been out of the question in the public schools. Schools have traditionally been limited to handling the symptoms of disease in students who are chemically dependent. Parents called in to discuss their youngsters' failures have listened to discussions about study habits. Schools have set up programs to teach those study habits. Counselors have sent out requests for evaluation of a student's progress and teachers have filled in their responses. Parents have asked for lists of unmade up work and then asked for progress reports about that work. Schools have wrestled with attendance policies which vary from no reporting of absences at all to policies which require telephone calls about every absence from class. Crises rooms, structured study halls, detention rooms — they've all been recommended. They've all been tried with initially high hopes that someone had finally come up with an answer. In most cases they have failed, at least a large part of the time. A general feeling of frustration and despair has prevailed and a lot of chemical dependency has gone untreated.

Not that teachers and administrators haven't known better. That knowledge has been there for quite awhile. And students and parents have known better, too, for quite awhile. A call to the principal's office followed a recognized pattern. The immediate problem was identified. A student had missed too many classes. A senior had failed to earn enough credits to graduate. A teacher had reported behavior problems that had to be discussed. Counselors had test scores to report, scores which too often indicated a level of ability much higher than the student was achieving. Then the discussion turned to study habits, lists of unmade up work, ways of earning the credits. Everyone left such a meeting relieved that it was over, but also secretly sure that it had all been pointless. The real problem had never been touched. The discussion had dealt with symptoms, but the disease was still not identified. Recording a high temperature doesn't cure the fever; identifying the presence of a tumor doesn't make it go away. Listing the symptoms has never cured the disease.

Everyone knew the disease was there, even if it wasn't talked about. And schools have had to handle chemically dependent students. That handling has usually gone one way or another. If the symptoms got too bad — if, for instance, students came to school high once too often — authorities simply threw the students out of school. That was one way to handle the problem. Just put it somewhere else, out of sight, and pretend that it would be taken care of. The other reaction — and this worked if students kept quiet about their behavior — was to pass youngsters along after a given period of time. That way the number of complaints stayed down. Not many parents sue school districts because their children aren't really learning anything.

Guilt, however, grows. Concerned school people know that every time a student is thrown out of school or is allowed to graduate without having earned his diploma, someone is deeply hurt. That student has been allowed to leave an environment in which he should have found some preparation for the future without having had the help he or she genuinely needs. Something has to change.

Schools are institutions well-suited to work this change because the nature of the relationship of school and community is unique. Very few other organized activities regularly cut across lines which group people. People belong to groups — neighborhoods, churches, company organizations, fraternal lodges, ethnic divisions, age divisions, country clubs, families — but these are all units which by their very nature tend to keep people to some extent separate from one another. Within the community, the school draws from all groups, or it touches close to those which it does not touch immediately. Many groups have done excellent jobs of developing programs for their members. Churches and business organizations have recognized the needs of their own people. But few of these groups are able to have the impact in an overall way which a school can have.

When a school has an organized program involving a number of people who are trained to recognize symptoms of chemical dependency, interviews such as the one which begins this chapter can be very productive. In such a school, the principal would be alerted to the heart of Wes's problem. Teachers who have learned to recognize patterns of behavior which signal trouble refer students to members of the staff who conduct chemical dependency work. Counselors review school records which may reveal erratic academic achievement and pass on their findings. Together these people consider the symptoms. The student is involved in these discussions. If the conclusion is chemical dependency, the next step should be some form of treatment.

With the support of trained staff people and with his own training and experience, a principal can then call parents. An interview under these circumstances can be very productive. In Wes's case, the interview was the first step toward Wes's involvement in the school's group program. In weekly discussion groups with other students who are either directly or indirectly involved with chemicals, and possibly involved in recovery from chemical dependency, he can get support for his own recovery. In addition, his father has decided to go into treatment and his mother has joined a support group for spouses of chemically dependent people. All three members of the family are making progress toward freedom from addiction.

Chapter Two

An Overview

"Not too many years ago, we'd catch a kid drunk or high and we'd bring him in, call his parents, chew him out and kick him out of school," said William Manning, the principal of Wayzata High School.

"Then one day, finally, we looked at what we had been doing and realized that was an awful way of treating kids that obviously needed help. That's where it began," he said.

Word got around that Wayzata was developing a program to try to deal with chemical dependency in the schools. Along that peculiar line of communication called the grapevine, speculation grew and requests for information began to come in. The paragraphs above introduced a newspaper article which came out in the spring of 1976 as part of the response to those requests. Community reactions to the speculation and to the newspaper article ranged from immense satisfaction that something positive was finally being done to absolute horror that schools should involve themselves in any way with the evils of drug abuse. Clearly, one of the major needs for the success of such a program is understanding and acceptance from the community. Staff people have to do a lot of public relations work, particularly in trying to ease the fear experienced by those who seem to feel that talking about symptoms will somehow spread the disease.

The number of requests for information which come from school boards and administrators indicates that school people welcome the possibility of a more effective handling of chemical dependency. Presentations like the following explain the concept behind the Wayzata program. They help to introduce the kind of change which young people have seen happening to others and which they want for themselves and their families. The interview was broadcast over station WAYL in Minneapolis in late summer, 1977. The interviewer's questions are still typical of those raised by people today looking for an overall understanding of the program. Dr. Manning's answers respond to the request for general information and indicate the areas with which those developing a similar program will need to be concerned.

What is the chemical dependency program at Wayzata?
That's a question! Do you want it answered in half an hour or ten minutes? The program was designed and begun about three years ago primarily out of *guilt* on the part of a few of us who were working in the school district. We were actually not doing anything about drug use. When I speak of drug use I am primarily speaking about alcohol use by our students at Wayzata High School. If kids came to school high, we would force them

out of the building. However, it suddenly dawned on us that what we were doing was taking our problems and pitching them out the front door without doing anything for the youngster.

Consequently, our entire program was designed around the concept of early recognition. We do not believe that we can prevent chemical abuse in our secondary schools, at least in Wayzata, or, I think, in almost any secondary school (junior or senior high school) in this modern society. We believe that we are a drug- and alcohol-using society. I guess that I have to elaborate and say that when I'm talking about chemical use I'm talking about the 90% of the chemical use centering around the drug ethyl alcohol. I guess I should revise that to say that 90% of the use centers around ethyl alcohol and pot or marijuana. The other 10% of use involves the exotic chemicals such as heroin, cocaine, the amphetamines, and the barbiturates.

We are dealing primarily with youngsters who are abusing themselves with alcohol. We are hoping that early recognition will be the best prevention of serious trouble. At the present time, as I've said, we don't believe we can prevent abuse entirely.

How do you go about preventing chemical abuse? Can the students come to you?
We have a program in the high school that is now being accepted by the faculty. It's important to recognize that you don't begin a program of this type if you intend to start with a program only for the students in school. We tried that for a year. We got some youngsters into treatment, began to confront some others on their chemical use, and spun our wheels for almost an entire school

year.

Then suddenly it dawned on us that for a program to be successful, that program must start at the top. What I mean is this: the people in a position of power — administration, faculty and even the public — must accept the concept that those people who are being hurt by the use of chemicals, even if they don't abuse chemicals themselves, are also involved in the disease. With that concept in mind, the next step is to convince faculty, boards of education, central office administration, and building principals that chemical dependency is a problem and that it's worthwhile looking at it. In order for a program to continue to work, that small group of people called Central Office and the Principals of the Buildings in the district must themselves take a look at the problem. So the concept begins at the top of the pyramid and ultimately it works down and reaches the students. It won't work if the role models and people at the top are not looking at the problem.

Taking a look at the problem is **not** what scares a lot of people, though. What does scare them is taking a look at their own use. We're not advocating prohibition. In the first place, I don't think it's possible to enforce prohibition of alcohol in the United States. It's just not possible. So, if you can't enforce prohibition — and I'm not in favor of that — then I think people have got to take a good hard look at why they use. We know, for example, that the greater share of students who are chemically dependent come from families with chemical problems.

We also know another thing, that probably the next largest group of students who are chemically dependent come from families who are total abstainers. Total abstinence is practiced in these families. What we are trying to say is that maybe we'd better take a look at the extremes in regard to chemical use and abuse. Maybe what we should teach our youngsters at an early age is responsible use. At Wayzata, we estimate, for example, that 97% of our students at the high school are on the line of either experimentation or abuse. Now, that's not to say that 97% of our students use regularly. I'm saying that someplace along the line, 97% of our students have had some chemical like alcohol or marijuana in their lives. It may be ceremonial wine at home or it may be complete drug abuse at the top level. Most are going to try. My own youngsters — four of them have gone through Wayzata High School — have told me that kids almost have to be weird not to experiment at least.

Now I know there are people who are going to be rubbed the wrong way by these statements, but I believe that we've got to be practical. If I were to ask you, "Would you like a drink?" you'd probably say, "No, we're on the air. We're taping now and I don't drink on the job."

But, I didn't mean it that way. I meant, "Would you like *something* to drink? Would you like a Coke, a cup of coffee, or even a glass of milk?"

In the public's eyes, taking a drink or having a nightcap means consuming some alcoholic beverage. If I were to ask you over to my house for a nightcap and then meet you at the door with hot chocolate, you'd probably think I was a little strange. So, that's the basis we start from. It's impossible to prevent use, and most people would say that it isn't even desirable to do so. When we begin at that level, then the program must center its attention on intervention — intervention when kids are really beginning to hurt themselves with chemicals.

When you talk about acceptable use and say 90% of the problem is with alcohol and pot, what do you mean by acceptable use?

When I talk about acceptable use, I'm not talking about pot. The evidence on permanent physical effects of smoking pot is not conclusive yet. We can't honestly tell kids that smoking pot is always dangerous to health. We must tell them, though, that smoking pot is illegal, and we have to emphasize that habitual use of a mood-altering chemical can be psychologically addicting. So we don't talk about using marijuana responsibly.

The use of alcohol, however, is a different matter.

I'm not a tee-totaler. I'm not chemically dependent. I believe that it's o.k. to have a drink. In no way am I going to stand up and publicly say that it's immoral, that it's sin, or that it's against all my beliefs. I'm a high school principal and I'm probably criticized by some people when I say it's o.k. to have a drink. By responsible use I mean people must use knowing there's no hurt coming out of their use. It's a rare phenomenon, but there are certain religions and certain countries in the world where there is very little abuse, very little dependency. I think one of the reasons that this is so is that families have been brought up to use responsibly. Certain religions use ceremonial wine. For these people there's nothing mysterious about chemicals.

The thing about chemicals, specifically alcohol, is that it will do pretty much what you want it to do. We learn, for example, that two beers will make us so high, three beers will do certain things for us. I ask a youngster, "Why do you smoke a joint or drink a beer?" The honest answer from that youngster, when he is willing to trust me, is, "A beer makes me feel better." It really does make them feel better. A couple of drinks make them feel better.

A couple of drinks make the adult society feel better. When adult society and youngsters today drink for the explicit reason of covering a problem, e.g., "I feel lousy today," "I'm looking ahead," "I deserve a drink," "I'm going to have one and when I have one I feel better about me," that's when drinking is really dangerous. It's dangerous when people use chemicals to alter mood. If you have a drink because it's a hot day and you've really perspired, if you drink a beer and it really tastes good, I think there's nothing wrong with that. I really don't. If it's a hot day and you drink eight beers because it's a hot day and because you want to get loaded, that's a different reason, and not a good reason.

Bill, how long have you been principal?
This is my twenty-ninth year at Wayzata. I began as a teacher, then I coached, became athletic director, assistant principal, and this is my fifth year as Principal. I've come up through the ranks. Wayzata is our home and our children have been raised here.

Your chemical dependency program in Wayzata has been in existence three years?
It's been in existence four years. The first year was the year we spun our wheels and tried to help kids and didn't take a look at the total school district, our own faculty, and our own administration. As I said, a program won't work if you continue the way that we started.

You've had quite a bit of experience, twenty-nine years, in the teaching business. You've been intimately associated with chemical dependency problems among students for

the past three years. How severe is the problem?
These are figures that you can gain from any organization
that gathers figures. I believe that in the United States
we're in the midst of an epidemic. We know, for example,
that there are ten to twelve million people who are
chemically dependent. We know that each one, on the
average, affects four other people among family members
or close friends. So, we have between forty and fifty
million people who are affected by the abuse of chemicals.
Roughly thirty billion dollars is lost in business each year.
We know that of the accidents which kill 56,000 people on
the highways in the United States, half are booze connected. Half of those responsible for the accident are chemically dependent. If we assume that an alcoholic is just as
likely as not to be the death victim in the accident, that
means one-quarter or 25% of those 56,000 dead were
chemically dependent people.

    We feel, for example, that the swine flu inoculation
inaugurated by President Ford was an example of the
national government's becoming panicky about a flu
epidemic. I thought it was a super thing. I took the shot. I
didn't want to get the flu. Yet we're sitting in the midst of
an epidemic that most people fail to recognize. It's a
problem which is probably the third leading killer in the
United States, next to heart disease and cancer. It's a
direct problem. It's something that can't be ignored. The
difficulty in understanding it is that it's a different type of
illness than we are used to. If an individual has cancer,
that person is operated on and goes through chemother-
apy. People gather together and they give much love and
concern to the sufferer and the family. But with the
disease of chemical dependency, more often there is
alienation. Ask the people who have chemically depend-

ent members of their families. They will tell you that very seldom is there a manifestation of love and concern by neighbors and friends. Usually there is a direct opposite, a splitting of the family.

I believe that chemical dependency is a problem that isn't going to go away. I also have another belief. I believe that prevention of alcoholism and drug addiction is going to be one of the greatest movements that ever came across secondary education in the United States. Minnesota, for example, has more beds per capita in treatment facilities than any other state in the Union. I am proud to say that, as far as I know, Wayzata has the first established school program ever in the United States to deal with the problem of chemical dependency. Since October 1, 1975, roughly twenty months ago, we have sent about one hundred-eighty-six students, forty-five parents, and twenty-three faculty members or members of faculty families to in-patient therapeutic treatment. That means they have gone into a hospital and stayed in the hospital, not been out-patients. Over two hundred of our community members have been involved in the treatment of chemical dependency as in-patients. Wayzata is a small suburban community with a school district of twenty-five to thirty thousand people. We're no different from any other suburban community.

Are you any different from the city?
No, I don't believe we are that either. I think that the cities may have different neighborhood problems. I know that it's vitally important for people who have been in treatment to come back and live in their community — to be role models — to say, "Hey, it really feels great to be free. It really feels great not to have to use."

Our kids who come out of treatment are probably the healthiest youngsters we have in school. They've quit using. They've taken a look at their own feelings, their own lives, and they've adjusted. They can say, "Hey, I really feel good about not using." That's very important.

You mentioned that chemical dependency is an *epidemic.* **When you use that word, you talk about a disease incidence that is high. You also said that the alcohol and drug abuse problem is a problem that we might never really overtake. Have we come up the hill now? Are we at a peak, unable to decline?**
I mean that a disease that affects one out of seven people is an epidemic. We may never overtake it because I think it's a problem that people are afraid to look at. No, I don't think we have reached the peak. I think abuse will continue to climb. As the population continues to increase, I think, the numbers of people with problems will increase.

Percentage wise?
I think the same percentages will prevail. We know, for example, that 12 to 15% of all people who use alcohol are going to become chemically dependent. That's one out of every seven. Those are national statistics. For any particular community, the figures might be a little different, but overall in the nation, out of every seven people who use, one is going to become chemically dependent. If, for every seven people who got up in the morning and had a cigarette, one was going to develop lung cancer, lung cancer would be classified as an epidemic. Unfortunately we have a tremendous amount of lung cancer, but I don't believe it develops in one out of every seven who smoke.

Maybe it does. I don't know those figures. One out of seven are the figures in chemical dependency and those are epidemic figures. If one out of every seven people who breathe the air was going to get swine flu, swine flu would be an epidemic.

We know that at least 25% of our population in the United States is affected directly by chemical dependency, either as an enabling member of the family or as a chemically dependent person. We know a few other things about which the American Medical Association agrees with us. The first is that chemical dependency is a disease. We believe that it's a primary disease. For example, a person doesn't drink because his wife doesn't like him. He may drink along with that feeling, but the disease is chemical dependency. And when his wife starts to like him, he will still be chemically dependent. If this person becomes chemically dependent in using, he can't truly blame it on the family relations. The second thing we know is that chemical dependency gets progressively worse. There isn't any way that a person who is chemically dependent can stay on the same level of use. There has to be an increase, depending upon the drug of his choice. The third thing we know is that chemical dependency is fatal. Persons who are chemically dependent are going to have their lives shortened. I guess with those things in mind and knowing the extent of use in society today, I would label this disease an epidemic. Yet I'm not thoroughly convinced that there's a way of preventing it. If we can prevent it, I believe it has to be done at a basic, elementary level with families. For honesty's sake, families have got to bring their children up saying, "Let's be open about our feelings."

Parents have got to teach their children that just

because it's a bad day, Mom doesn't drop a barbiturate. We don't take valium just because we've had a tough day. We don't take a sleeping pill because we've had a tough day. We don't come home from work and say, "Boy, I've really had a tough job today and what I really need and deserve is a drink!"

Our kids learn experientially. Learning in that manner, they say, "If I feel bad, it's o.k. to fix it with some chemical."

This is what I think we've got to teach our children: if we feel bad, we feel bad. We have to recognize the bad feeling and take care of the bad feeling or try to find some alternative that makes us feel good and not let that alternative be a chemical.

And that's the thrust of prevention?
Absolutely.

O.K., but how do you get directly at that? In theory it sounds good, but how do you put it into practice?
Well, it hasn't been in practice in many areas. We're beginning this fall to move toward the direction of practice. In this matter, I have to give a great deal of credit to several of our counselors at Wayzata High School for their work. The program would not be successful without them. This fall in one of our elementary schools we are beginning to teach parents and first graders and kindergarteners how to take care of feelings. We aren't even going to talk about chemicals. We are going to get a group of kids together with their parents and teach them how to say, "Hey, it's a swell day! Just look at the day, it's a super day." Or, "I really feel lousy today. My dog died."

All of those things are important. It's o.k. for kids to cry. Teach your kids that it's o.k. to cry. Parents, it's o.k. to cry. Teach your kids to be up front with their feelings. If a kid is upset and angry because Dad won't allow a night out, then recognize the anger for not being allowed to go out. If a kid is disappointed or hurt or jealous of a brother or sister, then let there be recognition of the jealousy and hurt and disappointment. If a kid is lonely and saddened because of the dog's dying, for example, then say, "It's o.k. We know you loved your dog and you'd like to cry. That's o.k."

We can't let our young boys be brought up hearing us say that it's unmanly to cry. We can't say, "Listen, young men don't express feelings. Bury it. It's o.k. to bury it. Just don't let anybody see you cry. Be a man about it."

All those things really start kids off on the way to becoming very sick. I think that where prevention is going to occur ultimately — and we're already doing a little of it — is in bringing those elementary youngsters together and encouraging them to say to their parents, "Hey, Daddy, and Mommy, I really feel bad today," or encouraging kids to take the risk of saying, "Daddy, you hurt me last night."

Do you pin the blame, then, for some of the alcoholism on this hiding of feelings? You said earlier that if a man can't get along with his wife and turns to alcohol, he can't really blame the family situation. What can he blame?
I don't think we have all the answers. It's obvious that we're in the embryonic stage of prevention and we don't have all the answers. I don't mean to imply that you can place blame anywhere. I think if you really deeply believe that one out of every seven people is going to become

chemically dependent, the blame has to be placed on alcohol or chemical abuse. A youngster comes into my office and I ask, "Why do you use?"

He says, "You'd use, too, if you had that teacher."

Or I ask, "Why are you in trouble?"

"Well," he says, "if you had an old man like I've got, you couldn't stand to go home either without a couple."

"Why are you in trouble in school?" Why are you in trouble at home?" "Why are you in trouble with your girl?" "Why are you in trouble with your grades?" "Why are you in trouble with your job?" "Well, because my home life is horrible."

We can't let people cop out. The real reason they are in trouble is that they abuse chemicals. They are the type of person who has become dependent and their use has become harmful. Pain results from their use. Some people can drink from now until the day of their death, and no pain comes from their drinking. At Wayzata, we have begun to modify the term *chemical dependency.* Along with it, we have begun to use the term *harmful involvement.*

Someone asks me, "Am I chemically dependent?" I wouldn't know. My question to them would be, "Have you ever had any hurt in your life? Has the chemical caused you hurt?"

Then I'd ask, "Have you and your wife had a good, solid, sound argument? (I think that's o.k., by the way; that's healthy.) Has the argument occurred because you have abused yourself with a chemical? Have you come home drunk on Friday night, missed supper, an appointment, a date to go out with your wife, and tried to find some other excuse, when the fact was that had you not been using you would not have had the problem?"

I don't think you can blame any of those things. I could give you classic examples of husbands and wives and children blaming each other.

"You'd drink, too, if this weren't true."

"You'd drink, too, if you had an old man like mine."

"You'd drink, too, if you had a husband like mine."

They go on and on — blaming, rationalizing. but that's not the problem. The problem is that certain people can not use. All people do not abuse when using, but certain people can't use at all without abusing.

Is it abuse if it causes trouble? How much trouble does it cause in the school? We've all seen the TV documentaries and read the articles. What's the truth?

Well, I believe the truth is that for a certain number of students, chemical dependency is costing them their education and their lives. I believe that we have a great deal of chemical use in schools. Those who are abusing are being harmed, not only academically but also in their relationships with peers. They are harmed right down the line with teachers, friends, and families. I don't believe they're doing it intentionally. I believe they're sick, lonely students who find no positive self-concept in any other way. They feel terrible about themselves. Their friends and their peers are using, and so they alter their mood, they go out and get high because their peers do it. They have negative feelings about themselves. Once again, I am not condemning the people who get high occasionally. I'm only saying that when pain results from getting high, we have to take a look at it. Getting high because of pain is happening, and I think it's happening more and more. I graduated from high school in 1944. Chemical use is a great deal different now from what it usually was in 1944.

Today, I think, society accepts chemical use. I might ask a parent, "How do you feel about your kid smoking dope?"

They go out of their minds. I say, "Do you care if your kid drinks a couple of beers?"

They say, "Well, boys will be boys. Girls will be girls."

Approval of alcohol use is the coming thing. So it's o.k. to drink a few beers, but to smoke a joint is absolutely unacceptable to some people. Yet, if you look on the addiction graph scale, drinking alcohol is far more often addicting than smoking marijuana. I don't want to imply that I'm approving the use of marijuana, nor do I want to legalize it. I'm only saying that we have to be rational about it. We're living in a drinking society. If a youngster smokes a joint, we shouldn't blow our minds if we're o.k. with his drinking a six-pack of beer.

Is there use right in the school? Is it enough of a problem that it bothers those who are straight or who can handle their use?
Yes, of course there is chemical use in school. The important thing is that today the attitude on the part of the school is different. I believe that the school used to throw users out. Now, we are saying to the kids who use chemicals, "We want you to take a look at your use."

There isn't a youngster who comes to school high that we know of who is not asked to take a look at his use. We may even force him to take a look at it through chemical dependency counseling. Now, I no longer think that there is that group of youngsters who use chemicals destroying classes. Yes, I think there is pot being smoked in school. There are kids dropping amphetamines or barbiturates or valium and librium. Yes, there is chemical use. I would just dare you to take from any community a random sample of the same number of adults that we have in our student population. In that sample you will probably find more abusers of chemicals than you will find in the random sample of the student population.

I think students are not much different from adults. I make the statement that students don't learn to use chemicals in school. They might have been forced by peer pressure to experiment in school. I would not minimize peer group pressure because it's really a strong pressure. If a youngster is with a good group of kids and they are all going to drink a six-pack of beer, it takes the exceptional kid to be able to say, "No thanks, guys, I'm just gonna sit here." He or she is going to try a beer. I really can't condemn a kid for that. Peer pressure is very strong. I think that what we as parents must recognize is that experimentation is going to happen. What we'd better do is be able to recognize when abuse begins to take place. Moreover, I believe that parents, if a time comes when they see their youngsters hurting themselves and abusing themselves with chemicals, have to take a good hard stand and say, "Look, you're abusing. We see it and you're going to do something about it."

This takes guts on the part of parents. Doing something may mean counseling. It may mean confrontation and being placed in a treatment center either by court order or by just personally picking the youngster up and saying, "You're going to treatment."

It's obvious that after young people are eighteen there needs to be a little different approach to the problem, and that approach is called *confrontation*. We describe confrontation as good hard love. It's easy to be nice to your kids and let them get by with things. And what's neat about that is that you as a parent never have to face the problem. The thing that's interesting is that many times parents don't want to confront their kids about the youngster's chemical use because what they really know deep down in their hearts is that if they do, they are going to have to take a look at their own use. That really scares them.

What about the program for parents? You mentioned that, on the one hand, among the chemically dependent students at Wayzata some come from families where the parents are themselves dependent. On the other hand, some of them come from families in which parents are very strictly against chemical use. What do you say to those people? It must be quite a shock to them to have their children involved.
I think it's a shock to both groups. It's traumatic for some parents even to think that their youngsters are experimenting. To the parents who don't use, it's more than a shock. I'm sure that they become angry. They question what they have done wrong as parents. We don't try to decide which group parents belong to. We've come to the conclusion that parents should be involved, and we have a great group organized. Perhaps I shouldn't say organized. We have a group of parents who meet regularly in the high school. They are not organized as people think school groups should be organized, with a chairman and a vice-chairman, secretary and money-raising schemes. They are a very loosely organized group of parents who have someone in their families — themselves or their children — with chemical dependency problems. When they come and meet as a group, they are really acting as a support system for each other and for their children. If a new family becomes involved, a child becomes involved.

If the new family is upset, we may suggest that they call Mr. and Mrs. Blank of this group. They're a unique group of people. They will go to a new family and say, "Hey, we've been there ourselves. These are some of the things that you can do to help yourselves. Why don't you come down and meet us and listen to some of the things that we've gone through? I'm sure that we can give you support. We can give you some direction."

It's a neat organization. It's an organization that is vitally needed, and yet, I think, it has to be operated within a loose structure. I think that once they achieve a basic organization, responsibility for doing certain things takes over, and they enjoy this. We have about twenty or thirty parents who meet regularly at the high school under this system. That group is just one small part of the program, but it's an absolute must, an essential part of the program, to have parental support, and they are giving this support.

Is most of your program voluntary? Participants are voluntarily there?

Well, no. Students don't volunteer. If a student comes to school high, he's in the program. He may resist the program and parents may tell us, "You aren't getting our student involved in the program. We refuse to let you."

Then our statement is, "That's fine, but the next time your youngster comes to school high, we're transporting him to the detox center."

We can do that by law without parental permission. If he's in school high and refuses to look at the program or his problem, refuses to go to counseling, or refuses to go to student support group and ultimately into treatment, then we're going to say to that parent, "O.K., everytime he comes to school high, we are transporting him to the detox center."

If we do it — and we've had to do it only once — then the kids and the parents know we're going to do it. It's an interesting note that, as the program began rolling, having their youngsters involved became less and less a threat to families. What we're saying to them is, "It's no shame to have a youngster who is sick with chemical dependency. You don't have to deny it or reject the youngster. We'll work on the problem together."

There should be no moral implications with this any more than there would be with a case of measles. That's the point that we're anxious to reach.

Does the dependent student volunteer?
No, absolutely not. The students become involved if they use in school. There has to be a consequence for that. The consequence used to be that students were kicked out. Often that was what many of them wanted anyway. The consequence now is that students who obviously are abusing themselves with chemicals must take a look at their use.

On the other hand a non-using student could say, "Gee, I've got a family problem. I would like to have my parents *take a look* at their chemical use." A student can then become involved in the program solely on the basis that he knows that his family is sick, that someone in the family is chemically dependent. We have an Alateen group and an Alanon group which meet in the community. The program is all-encompassing.

You have no trouble recognizing the problem when a student stumbles into school in the morning. But what

about recognizing it among families or among the students when they come to school sober?

I would like to mention the Johnson Institute here because that's where I had my training. Chemical dependency is described by them — and I'm a believer of this — as a family disease. If you have a chemically dependent member of the family, the rest of the family is also affected by the illness. These other family members deny a problem exists, and they build their lives on this denial. If the student is using chemicals but he doesn't come to school exhibiting the behavior that we recognize in the drunk lying in the street, we must then look for some other things that happen. Grades drop or there's an attendance problem. We know this: if a student is using, problems will begin to arise. The problems may not occur in school, but they will begin to happen somewhere. We believe that even if a youngster isn't using, but someone else in the family is, there are going to be significant problems. There are going to be some recognizable symptoms in the student if he has sick parents. One of the things we hope to do is to have all of our faculty become aware of the subtle symptoms, the little things that happen, the little cries for help that come from a student.

Unfortunately, we don't get them all, neither signs nor students. There are youngsters, I'm sure, walking in our building who have a chemical problem of which we are not aware. But even now, we are able to spot enough students with some kind of drug related problem to keep ourselves busy. All I can say is that I know that those youngsters, if they continue to abuse themselves with alcohol and other drugs, will surface some day, even if they are out of our building.

Just this past week I had three parents from outside our

school district call and want to send all their children to
Wayzata because they have a chemical problem with one
or more of their children. What they are saying to me is,
"Our school district is not doing anything. Can our
youngsters come to Wayzata?" They are also saying, "I
am now willing to recognize the problem in my own
family."

That's really a neat thing to have happen in the
community — to have parents be able to say, "Hey, my
kids have a problem" or "My husband is a drunk, and
I'm willing to take a look at it."

Being willing to talk about the problem is jumping a
difficult hurdle. In order to do the talking, people have to
be aware of the symptoms of chemical dependency. They
have to accept the reality of the problem and be willing to
take the risk of doing something about it. They have to be
concerned about the people who are involved. I guess the
two most important words to use are "risk" and
"concern." We've got to take a risk of shocking, possibly
even offending some people with this program and we've
got to be concerned about what's happening with the
people we love who are abusing themselves with
chemicals.

**I'd like to turn back for just a moment to something you
mentioned earlier. You said that** *prevention* **is the key
word in getting to the alcohol abuse problem. What can
you offer in the way of suggestions to people? What are
the danger signals? How do we prevent other people's
abuse?**
Well, that's a hard question. The first thing we must do,
and it is the most difficult, when we are talking about
prevention, is to look at our own use. It was alcohol use

for me, and I enjoyed social drinking. I have never used anything else. I took a look at my use and I saw it was not doing me any good, that I was beginning to abuse, that I was harmfully involved. In most instances, parents naturally want the best for their children. I would like all parents to take a look at their own use. If all parents did that, it wouldn't mean that they would have to quit using. It would mean that someplace along the line they should seek out people who are knowledgeable and ask, "Am I abusing?"

I have a classic example if you would like to hear it. One of our students was hurt at school. We called the mother, she called the father and urged him to meet her at the hospital. The injury wasn't serious, but she wanted him to meet her at the hospital. The father was discussing it with me later, and said, "You know what my first thought was? I thought, "Dang it, I'm not going to be able to meet George for that afternoon cocktail before I go home." But my next thought was, "That doesn't make any difference. My kid's hurt and he's at the hospital."

The unique thing was that that parent was immediately concerned because he wasn't going to be able to have that pre-meal cocktail on the way home. He asked me, "Do you think I've got a problem?"

"No," I told him, "I don't think you've got a problem, but I think that you recognize one of the danger signals of the problem. If this had been your wife asking you to stop and pick up two dozen ears of corn on the way home, it wouldn't have bothered you. You could have picked them up and still stopped at the bar. But this was a problem that needed your attention at the hospital immediately. You immediately became a little irritated that you weren't going to have that drink. You probably don't have a

problem, but I think you really should take a hard look at
the importance of drinking in your life. You're anticipat-
ing your drinking before other important matters. I can
recall times when we had a festive occasion and were
going out to eat. I can remember saying, "Well, what are
we going to have to drink tonight? A martini? Maybe I'll
have a manhattan."

All of a sudden I began to say to myself, "Wait a
minute. You don't anticipate going out with your wife and
having a nice meal. You're thinking about having a
martini or manhattan."

That kind of anticipation is a danger signal. Parents
who think like this should take a good hard look at their
use. In order to do this, it helps to be guided by someone
experienced.

**One last question. Has the lowered drinking age had any
effect?**
I can only give my opinion. I have no data on which to
base my statement. I think that lowering the drinking age
has allowed eighteen-year-olds to provide booze for
sixteen-year-olds, whereas before, twenty-one-year-olds
provided booze for the seventeen-and eighteen-year-olds.
I think that the eighteen-year-olds were getting it from the
twenty-one-year-olds. I have a son, a teacher, who is
twenty-seven. He indicated to me that booze was there in
the school and available elsewhere as well. I've had
youngsters come into the office and say, "I can get you
anything you want from booze to whatever." What really
hurt in lowering the age level was that it put a permission
type of thing in the hands of kids who are still in high
school. Eighteen-year-olds can go out and buy beer. It's
legal for them to have a couple of beers before they come

to school, whereas before it was not. However, I don't think that passing a law is going to prevent or create chemical dependency problems. In terms of school discipline, I don't think it has helped to lower the age, but I don't think it was extremely detrimental, if we are talking about increasing the rate of alcoholism.

Chapter Three

From Idea to Full Program

"You sure as hell have screwed up our family's drinking habits!"

One member of the community voiced his reactions to Wayzata's chemical dependency program in just those words. His tone of voice, however, was not critical. There may have been a little sorrow behind the words, the sorrow one feels as he relinquishes careless pleasures and accepts responsibility for his actions, but there was pride, too. The pride which people feel when they know they can control themselves or when they know they have overcome real threats to their well-being. That kind of pride is a cornerstone on which an individual can build a happy, integrated life; it is a vital force.

Staff members who deal with problem students in the high school know, however, that for many kids that kind of pride is almost out of reach. The student who is chemically dependent is usually condemned to failure in his attempt for such a future. For a long time, the policy was to regard this failure as a failure of the family, one which the school should not be expected to handle. But as the incidence of drug abuse grew and the reports from the United States Public Health Service began to recognize chemical dependency as the Number Three Killer, behind cancer and heart disease among American citizens, it became increasingly obvious to staff members at Wayzata Senior High School that alcoholism and drug abuse was not a problem which could be ignored.

The program at Wayzata actually had its beginning in the summer of 1974. It was, however, almost fourteen months before the plans were operable and before those involved thought that they really had something to offer the students. For years, the school administration had treated some kinds of problems with genuine concern and genuine respect for students' rights and dignity. For example, the law allowed schools to give advice to students with venereal disease. These students could easily and confidentially be referred to a facility which would treat the disease. There were girls who were pregnant and were able to receive advice and support from school authorities. The school cannot recommend abortion, of course, but it could intervene with the girl's parents, if necessary, to help a girl soften the impact of the message for her parents or to assist her in choosing whether to go to a center for pregnant girls or to receive homebound teaching. Such young women received the help. In every case, emphasis was placed on making it possible for youngsters to continue their schooling.

When guilt and concern about drop-outs forced school people to examine their treatment of other students, it became quite clear that there was a discrepancy between treatment of youngsters with other kinds of problems and treatment of students who were chemically dependent. Operating on a highly effective level in one area, the school was doing virtually nothing in another. The handling of chemically dependent youngsters was not aimed at getting them to continue their schooling. It was rather pointed toward getting those kids out of the building as soon as possible. The major administrative activity was an attempt to corral pushers within the building. Attention was directed at the exotic chemicals such as speed, cocaine, or the barbiturates. It was easy for all of us to believe that the kid who came to school drunk or high was using some form of those drugs.

Public attention approved this approach to the problem, and that approval reached the school in the form of a directive. The principal and the assistant principal continued to receive feedback from the public. "Keep drugs out of the school" was the order. Teachers echoed the order. "Get that kid out of my classroom." Getting the student out of the classroom might even occasionally require force, but it was considered a necessary force. There were very few complaints from the public. It was all in the name of virtue, wasn't it?

But underneath all of the surface satisfaction in the strong handling of a situation and the public approval of it, there was a deep-down, gut-level feeling on the part of a few of the high school staff that the situation should *not* be handled that way. In addition to the feeling of guilt, there was also the strong fear that a son or daughter of a staff member might come to school high.

There was also the growing recognition that a lot of those highs were coming not from the exotic drugs which the public condemned, but from alcohol, which the public did not condemn. For a time the uneasy feelings could be soothed with the assurance that the bad apple had to go to save the whole crate. But eventually there came a time when this conscience-salving technique didn't quell the uneasiness. There weren't a lot of users in school. They were out on the streets. The school had an excellent attendance record. The kids with chemical problems weren't around any more to spoil that.

It was obvious, however, that the drug problem had not really gone away; it was just outside the building and off the property. It was equally obvious that the drug education courses required by the State Education Department and by the Wayzata school administration were not highly effective in preventing drug use and abuse.

About that time, three staff members attended a summer session at the Johnson Institute. In that summer of 1974, the Institute, which is located next to the Wayzata school district, offered scholarships to the three of them as part of the Institute's interest in helping the school district deal with the problems within the school. It was this summer training which was the genesis of the program operating now. Those three staff members finished the summer session determined to do something about drug use in the school.

The first staff problem which had to be solved before school began in the fall of 1974 was that of where to get the time necessary to deal with students with problems that might be drug related. Staff members were not available under that year's budget or planning. Wayzata has the same kind of time and financial budget problems as any other district, but if anything was to be done, at least a short portion of each day had to be set aside for dealing with students in difficulty. The senior high principal decided that one staff member should be relieved part time to begin work on the program. This staff member, one of the three who had attended the summer session, was a Wayzata Senior High graduate who had come back to teach English. His involvement in the program was a significant factor in its success. He was relieved from his teaching duties for one hour a day, and he spent that hour looking at the problem of chemical dependency among students and attempted to deal with those students who came to school under the influence of some chemical. As the program developed that fall, his one hour a day blossomed into several hours, in addition to his four hours of classes. Many, many extra hours of his own time went into that first year of the program.

What we saw as successes occurred occasionally. Once in a while, a student would stop using. But there was never the advancement and the success that those teachers and administrators who were involved had hoped would really prove what they were doing as both correct and necessary. One example of the problem which continued was that students who came out of treatment were so threatened by the rest of the users in the building that they retreated into obscurity. Many times these students who had gone through treatment doubted that it was worth the effort required to maintain sobriety, particularly if that effort involved taking a lot of hassling from their peers.

Something was wrong, but it wasn't quite clear what that something was. A great deal of effort was being expended, but it didn't appear to be accomplishing a great deal. A few students had been reached, but nowhere near the number who needed help.

Once again staff members turned to the Johnson Institute. Their advice repeated some advice they had given earlier. A program can't begin at the bottom of the pyramid. It has to begin at the top. That was really frightening. The top of this pyramid was the central office administration and the Board of Education. These people had to be convinced not only that the program was necessary for students, but also that in order for it to work they themselves had to be contributors and role models. The organizing staff members were learning now what they had not known at the beginning. For a program to work, the top administrative echelon, including the superintendent, the Board of Education, and building principals, must be willing to take a look at their own chemical use. If they do not, students will not.

This is a frightening and threatening position to place people in. To any group of people interested in promoting a chemical dependency program this may seem to be an almost insurmountable barrier.

Our first step was to approach central office people about the possibility of doing an in-service workshop for the Board of Education and administration in the district. The question which came back was, of course, "Do we really have a problem?"

This question disturbed us. In amazement and some anger, we asked each other, "Didn't they know that there are approximately eighty million drinkers in the United States and that one out of every seven of them is chemically dependent? Didn't they know that the roughly ten million who are chemically dependent each affect the lives of four other people? Didn't they realize that fifty million lives were being affected? Didn't they know that one out of every three suicides in this country is someone with a chemical problem? Didn't they know that chances of suicide are fifty-eight times higher for those who are chemically dependent than for those who are not? Didn't they know that over half the people killed on the highways in the United States are in alcohol related accidents and that half of those killed are dependent? Where were they when all these facts were printed in the papers?" These were all questions that ran through the minds of the three men as they sought for a specific answer to the question, "Do we have a problem?"

If they wanted to begin a program, however, they had to prove that Wayzata did have a problem. The first step was to develop a quick survey of all the students in the high school. It was, admittedly, a non-scientific survey which had to be given without ample opportunity to develop an atmosphere of trust among students. In some cases the answers were not even worth reading. But even with these problems, survey results indicated that a great number of Wayzata students were smoking pot and drinking alcohol.

Very few admitted the use of hard core drugs or exotic chemicals. The report, however, was enough to take back to administration. With it went a request for an in-service workshop for administration, the Board of Education, and building principals during the spring of 1975. The workshop was to be taken out of the ordinary work day, in order to reduce resistance to the plan. The organizers had contacted some of the board members and had been given assurance that they would come to the workshop. They had contacted the Johnson Institute to arrange for six hours of training time. With this arrangement came a figure as to cost. The request for that amount of money went to the proper authorities. This time the answer which came back was, "We don't have the money budgeted for such an expense."

When budgets are strained to their limits, as school budgets often are, the question of money is always a difficult one. Certainly no department budgets had surpluses to be diverted for this use. But an answer will usually occur to determined organizers. In this case the answer was to spend money out of pop machine funds. Profits from pop machines in the buildings had not been allocated for any other purpose. Here was an obvious need. Manipulating those funds toward the workshop required some soul-searching. What would the auditors say? But the workshop was a success in introducing the disease concept of chemical dependency, describing the progress of the disease, and generally getting across the attitude that it was o.k. to be sick.

At the end of the workshop there were many positive reactions, yet there were several of those who had been involved who still showed resistance to developing a program. Questions such as these were asked: "Do we dare to go into the personal lives of our faculty members, our students, and their families?" "Is it really any of our business whether people are using as long as they are producing well on the job?" "Do we have a right to talk to a student concerning what is happening outside the normal school hours?" "Do we even have a right to be involved in the lives of our students if those students come to school slightly intoxicated?"

All of these questions brought a great deal of frustration to those who really wanted to promote the program. Frustration often turned to anger. That anger led to more questions. "If we are willing to give our time to attempting to start a program," they asked, "why are so many road blocks facing us?" It took a great deal of time, a softening of anger, and a development of real understanding to realize that for many of those who were building road blocks the real fear was this: "If this program begins, what is it going to mean to me? Am I going to be part of it? Will I be driven to look at my own use?"

It is significant that even among those interested in organizing the program, for most, this last question was also frightening. Among those persons originally involved, only one was really secure. He was one, himself chemically dependent, who was now living a life free of chemicals. He was secure within himself and consequently was not threatened by the implications of the program.

With the first hurdle, the in-service for administration, successfully passed, the next challenge was to move on to the community and the faculty. This in-service attempt was to go to the committee planning the beginning workshop for the 1975-76 school year. Workshop week in the Wayzata School District is the week prior to the beginning of the school year, and it is important because much emphasis is placed on beginning the year with a strong, positive attitude. Workshop week is always cluttered with meetings — building meetings, district meetings, department meetings. Department heads meet. Guest speakers are invited. Some things go on which are not particularly relevant to the beginning of school.

On the whole, however, the week is productive and does, in most cases, accomplish the task of arousing enthusiasm and good feeling about the coming year. It was a very difficult thing to convince the committee planning the workshop for that fall of 1975 that it would be valuable to give a full afternoon program to the problems of chemical dependency. With the help of administrative pressure, however, the afternoon was set aside. Schedules for workshop week went out to all faculty members, to district personnel, and to the Board of Education. Response to those schedules left no doubt that there was a great deal of dissension among the staff about time allotted to learn a little bit about chemical dependency.

The first in-service workshop was planned just to provide the staff with a very clear-cut picture of the character of chemical dependency as it relates to situations at work and among families. Such a picture is clearly applicable to the classroom and to one's family and one's self. The best way to present this picture seemed to be through the use of the film *I'll Quit Tomorrow*, produced by the Johnson Institute.

The film is an excellent vehicle for transmitting the disease concept of alcoholism and for displaying the family illness which results when one member is a victim of dependency. The film can easily be divided into three parts. Each portion can be used to promote discussion of aspects of abuse. The film is a touching story which illustrates the background of dependency as well as the confrontation and intervention which can lead to treatment.

The workshop with the board and administration had taught a few lessons about introducing the program. The organizers of this faculty presentation wanted the faculty to understand what really happens in the disease of alcoholism. *They firmly believed that it is a disease best learned about experientially.* The most productive way for a person to truly learn about the progress of the disease is for that person to examine his or her own use. For the non-user this can be difficult and possibly can only be done by listening to and learning from someone else. Dr. Manning would liked to have shared the follow-

ing with the faculty. At the time, it did not seem
appropriate to do so. He shares it at this time.

"It wasn't until I personally became involved in the
chemical dependency program that I realized how my
own life had followed the pattern which the AMA had
outlined as the progress of the disease. My children had
learned from me as one of their leading role models. I
came from a family where abstinence was not only
preached but practiced. There was no chemical use in my
immediate family as I grew up. As an only child, I was
taught that one's physical body was precious and that one
did not abuse it with alcohol. I was greatly involved in
athletics as a youngster, and training rules were committed to abstinence. At that time, during the early 1940s,
there was not so much observable use of alcohol among
young people, and peer pressure for use was not so great.

"My first experience with alcohol came during World
War II when I was inducted into the armed forces. I had
never had anything to do with alcohol, and it remained a
great mystery. I had listened to a lot of tall tales about the
things that happened if you drank, perking up when I
heard how easy it was to seduce your girl if she had been
drinking. I heard that people who used alcohol could do a
lot of things that those of us who didn't use just couldn't
do. I heard that alcohol contributed to a lot of good times.

"It all sounded pretty exciting, so the first thing I did on
my first evening at Fort Leavenworth, Kansas, after my
induction was go to the PX and order a bottle of beer. I
was embarrassed that I didn't know a local brand, but I
drank one bottle and then another and got pretty high,
discovering the magic the kids had talked about. One beer
made me dizzy; two would do a lot for me. I discovered
that a couple of bottles of beer could be pretty pleasant,

and I didn't suffer any pain from these lessons. If we had a really bad day or if a sergeant gave me a bad time, I could count on a couple of beers at the PX to make me happy again and help me forget the things which had given me the bad time.

"My drinking continued over a number of years. I ultimately learned that martinis would take me to the point when my nose would become numb, and I learned that any more after that point would certainly bring pain. That pain was not only the physical pain of a hangover, but it was also the emotional pain which resulted from doing things contrary to my upbringing or to my ethical code. After I married and as my children grew, I also, as I realize now, taught my children that the use of chemicals would solve problems, or at least ease the pain of problems. I never physically abused my wife or children. But as my use continued through the growing responsibility of my jobs as teacher, coach, assistant principal and finally principal, I taught them experientially that the use of a chemical could be a good thing.

"As an assistant principal, I had a very difficult job. In the eyes of many people in education, the assistant principalship is one of the worst positions in a school. He gets all the dirty details. Attendance and discipline are usually his responsibility, along with all the tasks the principal himself doesn't want to do. I hope this is changing. I don't honestly believe that this was always true, but there were many times when I felt that it was the case, and I did use my feeling as a reason to drink.

"Very rarely did I drink during the week, but on Friday night, if we were not going to a school function, the children learned to stand back a ways. They knew their Dad had had a rough week. I convinced them that mine was the toughest job in the world. If they had to deal with the kids and parents and administration I had to deal with, I informed them, they would understand my need for a drink or two on Friday night.

"I liked to have my weekend planned socially. It became more and more important, too, that those plans should involve alcohol. I believed that I *deserved* a drink, or better two or three drinks. My children saw me come home irritable. They saw that after a couple of drinks I became quite cheerful. In this way, over the period of years during which they were growing up, I taught them that alcohol was an acceptable way to relieve feelings of anger, guilt, loneliness, or frustration. I showed them it worked. It worked every time.

"As I progressed during those drinking years, if it had not been for a very, very strong wife, I might have had a chemical problem. My wife Bettie and the chemical dependency program here at school have been the two strongest deterrents to that potential dependency. I was at a very dangerous position in my drinking life. At that point the program made me take a hard look at my own use and my relationship to my own family. I decided that the chemical was beginning to be detrimental and I was beginning to use it for the purpose of altering my mood. I believe that I saw the beginnings of alcohol abuse and the early sprouting that could grow into the disease."

This testimony of Dr. Manning's would, however, have been premature for the whole group at this early date. Programs and people need time to grow. During this introductory period, experiences were shared more personally, more privately.

The conviction which an individual develops from experiences, however, can be passed on to others, and it was this conviction which Dr. Manning did share. The first workshop for faculty was, generally speaking, a successful experience.

Most of the staff members attended the session. There were, however, a couple of instances which the organizers had not yet anticipated, and which indicated unwillingness among a few teachers to look at their own use. One man was very insistent that teachers should not have to watch the film. There was too much school business to be attended to, he said. Stock inventories had to be taken, a mail delivery had come in that morning, equipment in his department had to be attended. He had an appointment with someone who was due to arrive at any time. It finally became necessary to say to this person, "This is a part of workshop week. You will come to this part of the program."

Another faculty member had a more covert way to avoid involvement in the session. During the first reel of the film, one of the organizers of the program noticed a small light being flashed in the darkened auditorium. The light turned out to be a small penlight flashlight. This teacher had placed himself in the back of the room in such a way that he could use a flashlight to read a pocketbook edition of a new novel. Those in charge of the program had to pass this off as an instance of an individual's setting his own priorities. It was obvious to them, however, that this person was afraid even to watch a film on dependency. There were also some unexpected positive results.

This first workshop brought about one faculty member's examination of a family situation. As a result that teacher's spouse was committed to a hospital for treatment. If such could result from one four-hour workshop with one school district faculty, how many people would be touched when the program really got under way? The organizing group was enthusiastic enough about this first step to request a second two-hour block of time. Central office was receptive, but there was no time available.

Despite a shortage of time, follow-up was necessary. Elementary principals requested that their faculties come to after-school workshops. Teachers agreed. Secondary school principals decided to go about it a little differently. Each of the principals divided his staff into thirds. The division placed one-third of each department in each group. Group A of a given department attended a workshop for two hours on one morning while Groups B and C shared the responsibility for covering Group A's classes. The next morning Group B attended the workshop while the other two groups covered the classes. The third morning Group C had its workshop session. In this way each principal was able to arrange an additional two hours in-service training.

Central office administration was now convinced that an additional half-day should be provided for still another follow-up, and this half-day came from released time for students. The three sessions together added up to a ten-hour workshop of in-service training for all faculty members. Out of this final session came a question from another faculty member which resulted in a commitment from staff to intervene with the abuse of chemicals by the spouse. Again the organizers felt encouraged. "What will happen," they asked themselves, "if we can really get people to feel good about themselves and to become role models for our students?"

The next step was to turn to in-service for non-certificated staff and their families. Then came presentations to all of the service clubs in the school district. Elementary PTA programs focused on the problem. Churches asked for presentations.

The question of a presentation to the senior high school PTA was a knotty one. Organizers debated whether to inform parents of the nature of the program. The decision was not to do so, but to make a special push for attendance. Each member of the high school staff was given twenty-five names of parents to call personally. Each call issued a special invitation to a very special meeting. Out of a possible 3,200 parents eligible to attend, about 1,200 came to the meeting. This was far and above attendance at any previous meeting.

The evening was spent in just describing the disease of alcoholism. Program organizers talked about their hope for the future. They showed the first reel of *I'll Quit Tomorrow*. The next morning at 7:00 a.m., standing at the door of the principal's office when he arrived, were three families who proved the value of the meeting. After becoming involved the night before, they had decided after they had gone home and talked it over, that within their families they had a problem with chemical abuse. They wanted suggestions as to what they could do, and they wanted to get started on those suggestions.

Through that first PTA program, counselors were able to get three more people into successful treatment. Since the actual beginning of the program in the fall of 1975, members of over 20,000 residences within our school district have taken part in education on alcoholism and drug dependency.

And as one member of the community has said, with just a little touch of regret and with a great deal of pride,

"You sure as hell have screwed up our family's drinking habits!"

Chapter Four

Policy, Philosophy, and Finance

Ten and twenty dollar bills lay in a neat pile on Dr. Manning's desk. "We want you to use this for your chemical dependency program," the woman said. "I don't want a receipt," she went on, "and my husband and I prefer to remain anonymous."

She had called earlier for an appointment one August morning. Late in that summer of 1975 the program in the Wayzata Senior High School had been underway for a year, but it had been an unsatisfying year. No money had been specifically designated for a program designed to help students who were harmfully involved with drugs, and for the past school year only one individual had been free to work with those students on anything like a regular basis. Looking at the work, some results promised success, but those results had been largely due to hours and hours of one man's time, developing out of one class hour each day set aside from his regular teaching assignment in the English Department. Word of the effort, however, had reached this family.

"This is some profit my husband and I received recently. We'd like to share it with you on the condition that it be used in your chemical dependency program."

She explained that she and her husband were both chemically dependent. Out of their experiences had grown their recognition of the value of a program designed to intervene in dependency in young people. This recognition had prompted them to share a windfall. The gift amounted to $650.00, freely given for use in the school's program.

The value of that gift, however, was much greater than $650.00. As an expression of confidence from people who really understood the significance of prevention, it acted as a tremendous boost to those who were organizing the program. Here was an indication that community support could be expected, and anyone who has ever been involved in public school programs knows that the presence or absence of community support is often the deciding factor in the success of those programs.

As a community, Wayzata has a tradition of being involved in its schools. The city itself is not large. Its population in 1976 was about 3,700. And the area of the city is not large. Surrounded by a number of other communities, Wayzata has no opportunity for growth in area. However, the city of Wayzata is only a small part of the Wayzata Public School District, with parts of eight other communities lying within the district boundaries. Approximately thirty-eight square miles make up the area served by the school.

For many people, the name Wayzata carries connotations of wealth. The city is built along the shores of Lake

Minnetonka, west of Minneapolis. In the closing years of
the nineteenth century, the lake was famous as a resort
area, and families from as far as St. Louis came to spend
their summers on its shores. Large resort hotels served
those people in the 1880s, but gradually the lakeshore
was sold for private homes. Early owners gave their
names to islands and bays of the lake. Spacious homes
were built by members of flour and lumber families and
the area gained a reputation for affluence.

That affluence, however, is only one small portion of
the Wayzata School District and, indeed, is but one part
of the total effect. The children who grow up in the largest
homes along the lake often attend private schools within
the state or go east to boarding schools. The public school
population draws from a broad range of incomes and
occupations.

In 1972 a committee from the school and the community evaluated the occupational status of adults in the
district and determined that a little over 50% of those
adults were in occupations loosely categorized as white
collar. The population is, like many other suburban
communities, fairly mobile, but the same 1972 report
indicated that about two-thirds of the students in the
district had attended Wayzata Schools for more than half
of their schooling. Seventy percent of the seniors of that
year had been in the Wayzata system for at least six years.
These figures indicate some degree of stability.

Studies of senior classes in the past several years show
that somewhat over half of the class plans to go to college
and an additional 15-20% expect to study in some
program beyond high school. These figures are not
particularly remarkable. They are quite similar to statistics for other suburban schools.

In addition, Wayzata is not particularly remarkable in its history of drug abuse. Students at Wayzata probably do not use chemicals appreciably more or less than do their peers in other high schools across the country. Although teachers and parents are often dismayed over the problems which drug abuse gives rise to, the problems are not more spectacular here than they are anywhere else.

The area in which Wayzata has been remarkable, however, has been in the organization and promotion of the program designed to deal with student and faculty abuse of chemicals. Because the board has adopted a policy for treatment and because the program used in our school has been widely discussed, the impression has developed of a community in which abuse is wide-spread. This wide-spread abuse is, of course, no more true in Wayzata schools than it is in most other schools. What is more wide-spread here is the degree of concern and the desire to provide treatment for those who are harmfully involved. The first important step in recovery for an individual is for him to accept that he is powerless over alcohol, that his life is unmanageable and that *some* form of treatment is his only alternative. The first important step in community programs is for the community to accept that there is a part of itself that has lost control over chemical use and which part requires treatment. Harmful involvement with chemicals can not be handled in a hush-hush way. Open, healthy discussion must occur for recovery to happen. Moral judgments, refined niceties, and dislike for unpleasant topics must all be put aside and replaced with willingness to recognize a problem and to cooperate in a community effort to deal with it.

In the Wayzata School District Central Office, building

principals and school board members worked together to develop a district philosophy and policy which would provide treatment for all individuals who are part of the school community. Verbal support is fine, but official policy — specific statements of expectations and goals — is vital.

District policy views chemical dependency as a problem which affects 10-20% of all people who use any mood-altering chemicals. The official position of the school is that schools are in a uniquely favorable situation to address this problem helpfully. The most desirable goal, of course, is prevention. The statement of philosophy recognizes, however, that absolute prevention of chemical dependency is an unrealistic goal. The role of the school must rather be to provide education and to participate in early recognition and intervention when students become harmfully involved.

Under the district policy, education includes information on both exposure, risks, and symptomatology. The purpose of this education is to enable individuals to evaluate experiences with mood-altering drugs. Emphasis is on the primary perspective of physical and emotional health rather than on moral concerns.

The district does not think that the schools should be treatment facilities. They are, rather, cooperating agents working with treatment centers, halfway houses, and other social agencies. The schools act primarily through referral and support. If students or employees become harmfully involved, the district expects to provide reasonable assistance in easing this involvement. This assistance will take the form of evaluation, treatment referral, and counseling. In order to provide this help, the district must have an adequate staff well trained in education, evaluation, intervention, and support not only by students but also by staff and parents as well. The intention of this program is to enhance the basic educational mission of the schools.

The district believes that a chemical dependency program should not distract or divert any emphasis from that basic educational mission of the schools. However, the district also contends that to ignore the problem or to deal with it only in a punitive way would diminish overall instructional effectiveness. The nature of harmful involvement is such that it may be dealt with daily in some way or other. The Wayzata School philosophy simply suggests that harmful involvement must be dealt with appropriately. This belief led to the formal adoption of the following philosophy, policy, and procedures.

Wayzata School District 284
Philosophy on Chemical Dependency

Alcoholism and drug abuse are two of today's major health problems resulting in increased human tragedy and economic loss. The Wayzata School District recognizes chemical dependency, including alcoholism, as a treatable disease which can be permanently arrested. Harmfully dependent people can be returned to productive, healthy lives. The social stigma often associated with this disease only increases the suffering of the chemically dependent and their families.

The Wayzata School District has engaged the Johnson Institute of Minneapolis to assist in training Wayzata personnel in the identification and understanding of the disease. The Institute offers counseling and referral services for any employer or family member who wants assistance. All contacts with the Johnson Institute will be on a confidential basis.

The confidential nature of the medical records of employees with chemical dependency, including alcoholism, will be preserved in the same manner as all other medical records. A person who suffers from this disease will also receive the same employee benefits and insurance coverage provided for other diseases under our established employee health insurance plans.

Wayzata Independent School District 284 Health Policy on Chemical Dependency

Wayzata School District 284 recognizes chemical dependency as a treatable illness. District employees who are so diagnosed shall receive the same consideration and opportunity for treatment which is extended to employees with other types of illnesses. Employees with the illness of chemical dependency shall qualify for the same employee benefits and group insurance coverages which are provided for other medically certified illnesses with established employee benefit plans and programs.

The District is concerned about the effects which harmful chemical involvement has on the employee's job performance and personal health. For purposes of this policy, *harmful involvement* occurs when an employee's consumption of mood altering chemicals repeatedly interferes with the employee's job performance or personal health.

Supervisors will implement this policy in such a manner that no employee with chemical dependency will have his/her job security or promotional opportunities affected either by the diagnosis or by the employee's own request for treatment.

The confidential nature of the medical records of employees with chemical dependency will be preserved in the same manner as for all other medical records.

The administration is directed to develop procedures for the implementation of this policy.

Procedures for Intervention in Chemical Dependency Cases

1. When harmful chemical use is indicated there shall be a consultation among building principal, a chemical dependen-

cy counselor, and any other concerned persons for data sharing.

2. If, as a result of preliminary consultation, direct action is indicated, there shall be a consultation or intervention with the employee. The principal, a chemical dependency counselor, and other concerned persons will be present.

3. When the above group determines action is necessary, the employee is expected to accept the recommendation of the group to follow one of the following procedures:

   a) inpatient treatment at an approved facility and active involvement in A.A.

   b) outpatient treatment at an approved facility and active involvement in A.A.

   c) successful and active involvement in an A.A. program.

   d) other involvement in an acceptable rehabilitation program.

If an employee doesn't consent to the recommendation of the group, he/she will be required to submit to a physical examination by a physician who is competent at the expense of the school district. Refusal to submit to this examination may result in immediate discharge. (See Sec. 125.12, Subd. 7 "Suspension and Leave of Absence for Health Reasons," and Sec. 125.12, Subd. 8f "Immediate Discharge" of Minnesota Statutes.)

Sec. 125.12, Subd. 7 SUSPENSION AND LEAVE OF ABSENCE FOR HEALTH REASONS Affliction with active tuberculosis or other communicable disease, mental illness, drug or alcoholic addiction, or other serious incapacity shall be grounds for temporary suspension and leave of absence while the teacher is suffering from such disability. Unless the teacher consents, such action shall be taken only upon evidence that suspension is required from a physician who has examined the teacher. The physician shall be competent in the field involved and shall be selected by the teacher from a list of three provided by the school board, and the examination shall be at the expense of the school district. A copy of the report of the physician shall be furnished the teacher upon request. If the teacher fails to submit to the examination within the prescribed time, the board may discharge him, effective immediately. In the event of mental illness, if the teacher submits to such an examination and the examining physician's or psychiatrist's statement is unacceptable to the teacher or the board, a panel of three physicians or psychiatrists shall be selected to examine the teacher at the board's expense. The board and the teacher shall each select a member of this panel, and these two members shall select a third member. The panel shall examine the teacher and submit a statement of its findings and conclusions to the board. Upon receipt and consideration of the statement from the panel the board may suspend the teacher. The board shall notify the teacher in writing of such suspension and the reasons therefor. During the leave of absence the teacher shall be paid sick leave benefits by the district up to the amount of his unused accumulated sick leave, and after it is exhausted, the district may in its discretion pay him additional benefits. The teacher shall be reinstated to this position upon evidence from such a physician that he has made sufficient recovery and is capable of resuming performance of his duties in a proper manner. In the event that the teacher does not qualify for reinstatement within twelve months after the date of suspension, his continuing disability may be a ground for discharge under subdivision 8.

Sec. 125.12, Subd. 8f IMMEDIATE DISCHARGE
A school board may discharge a continuing-contract teacher, effective immediately, upon any of the following grounds:
- (a) Immoral conduct, insubordination, or conviction of a felony;
- (b) Conduct unbecoming a teacher which requires the immediate removal of the teacher from his/her classroom or other duties;
- (c) Failure without justifiable cause to teach without first securing the written release of the school board;
- (d) Gross inefficiency which the teacher has failed to correct after reasonable written notice;
- (e) Willful neglect of duty; or
- (f) Continuing physical or mental disability subsequent to a twelve months leave of absence and inability to qualify for reinstatement in accordance with subdivision 7.

Non-certificated employees will be accorded the same provisions as outlined in Sec. 125.12 Subd. 7 and 8 under Minnesota Statutes for certified employees.

Wayzata Independent School District No. 284
Student Health Policy on Chemical Dependency

District 284 Schools recognize that chemical dependency is an illness often preceded by misuse and abuse. Because District 284 wishes to intervene early in the disease process, contact with students manifesting signs of misuse or abuse will be made to both educate and aid them should they need help.

Initial contact will be made after a referral source alerts the chemical dependency staff. Referrals come from a multiplicity of sources demonstrating concern — parents, teachers, friends, concerned students, administration, law enforcement, courts, social workers, and school counselors.

Referral sources will remain confidential until after initial contact is made with the student and parent or guardian.

Students who do not have a chemical problem may wish the aid of the chemical dependency staff and program in supporting their decision not to use at all. Such support is available through the chemical dependency program.

Other students may have a parent, guardian, or significant person who has a chemical problem; help is also available for them through the chemical dependency program.

The District believes that if a student is involved in the chemical dependency program and successfully addressing his/her harmful involvement with chemicals, he/she may continue in the regular school setting and continue to participate in any special programs, *i.e.*, athletics, Focus, Contact, special education, *etc.*

When a student is recommended to the chemical dependency program for evaluation, all information will be kept confidential and shared only with involved staff and the student's parents.

The following procedure is recommended when a referral is received:

1. The chemical dependency counselor will contact the student for an initial interview of one or more sessions. The counselor may also contact other concerned persons at this time to confirm or amplify data received.
2. After the initial interview, the chemical dependency counselor will inform the principal and the regular school counselor of the recommended course of action for the student, which would be one or more of the following:
   a) would benefit from more knowledge of harmful drug consequences, therefore suggest four weeks of group involvement in chemical dependency program.
   b) further evaluation in chemical dependency group necessary — four weeks in group.
   c) inpatient treatment — needs intervention.
   d) outpatient treatment — may need intervention.
   e) active A.A. involvement.
   f) no problem, no immediate concern.
3. The chemical dependency counselor will then contact the student's parents and inform them of the recommendation. He/She should also solicit their active support for these recommendations.

4. The regular school counselor should contact the parents also and recommend contact with any existing parent support groups within the school or community.

The student's resistance to group, treatment, or A.A. will probably be high; therefore it is important that parents be made aware of the child's needs for help.

In cases where neither the student nor the parents will cooperate in taking steps to intervene in a student's harmful involvement with chemicals, his/her position in school might be in jeopardy. Factors to be taken into consideration when his/her position becomes critical are as follows:
1. Is the student using in school?
2. Is the student's chemical use adversely affecting his/her behavior in school?

3. Does the student refuse to participate in any school chemical
   dependency programs or approved chemical dependency
   programs in the community?
4. Is the student's continued involvement with chemicals harmful to other students?

Districts beginning similar programs may discover that
developing an official statement of policy and procedures
is extremely difficult. Another school district once asked
staff people from Wayzata to assist in setting up their
program. The major roadblock seemed to be wording of
policy. Careful analysis finally indicated that the concern
over wording was actually masking a much deeper
concern over touching in any way a problem so sensitive
as district involvement in chemical abuse. Once again
Wayzata's program organizers were convinced that educational programs aimed at facing people's fears must
precede writing policy. An atmosphere of trust is the first
necessity.

Finances can be the second roadblock in a school
district about to begin a program of this type. Here again
fears and unwillingness to take a risk can bring about
obstacles that seem legitimate. It is difficult for school
administrators to look at chemical dependency and budget for it. Visualize what a school district would do if one
of its cooks were to come down with infectious hepatitis
or if a home economics teacher were to develop acute
tuberculosis.

A classic example of how people take a very serious
disease and budget money to prevent or cure it was
President Ford's program for innoculation against swine
flu. With chemical dependency, we are in the midst of an
epidemic which involves the third leading killer in the
United States. At Wayzata, as in many other schools, we

believe that 97% of the students are somewhere on the line between experimentation and abuse with chemicals. This does not mean they are or will become addicted, but the possibility of addiction for many of them is high.

People do not like to face this type of issue. They find all kinds of excuses to skirt it and one of the excuses that is most often used is, "There just isn't enough money." In the summer of 1975, the Wayzata program began with $200.00 taken from the pop machines in the building. These funds were diverted from their normal use in order to provide funds for the first administrative workshop. That same summer, Wayzata's principal received the $650.00 donation. These funds were the total financial beginning of the program.

The next problem was to get the Board of Education to agree to a budget, a budget designed to include training and confidential counseling for staff members and their families. Because it was necessary to substantiate the need, once again it was necessary to teach about the national statistics. Once again it was necessary to attempt to get the board and central office to understand the problem of chemical dependency. The Johnson Institute offered scholarships to help. Finally after a great deal of effort, the Board of Education agreed to a budget of $2,500 for the 1975-76 school year. It was another beginning.

The sum provided a three-week training course for six faculty members at three-week courses at the Johnson Institute. It also included $500 for individual and personal counseling for staff members. The money was not, however, sufficient. The program required a great deal of work on a voluntary basis. There were times when its organizers indulged in a little self-pity and there were times when they felt unwilling to contribute any more. Yet there were successes with students and with parents, and the occasional successes kept the program moving.

During the spring of 1976, organizers had sufficiently demonstrated need and a budget was presented to the Board of Education. This budget requested training money plus additional staff time for the 1976-77 school year. At the same time the Minnesota State Legislature had approved a bill allotting over a million dollars to research the problem of chemical dependency in the state. The school board expressed an understandable interest in applying for some of that money. Those responsible for the program documented the need and made proper application. In May of 1976, the state department of education notified the district that, while it was to be complimented on the program, the money was denied. This was a high school program that, as far as anyone knew, was non-existent anywhere else. This was a program that had demonstrated success in a first year of operation with over forty people brought into treatment. No other school district had publicly initiated a program of this type by admitting that problems of abuse existed.

Readers who made the decision about funding, however, indicated that they did not feel that the program was innovative. Instead, those readers only encouraged continued teaching about harmful effects of drug abuse. For years, the Wayzata School District had followed the state law requiring instruction in both eighth and tenth grades on the harmful effects of tobacco, drugs, and alcohol. But those classes aimed at prevention were not successful in preventing abuse. Experimentation continued; harmful involvement was not being prevented.

Denial of state money meant that funding must be

local. It was a measure of the effectiveness of the education, of the enthusiasm of the organizers, and of the courage of the board that the budget request was approved.

Money was set aside for the Johnson Institute for counseling and workshops. Staffing was provided at the three secondary schools. Wayzata Senior High was given one counselor working full time and one working four-tenths of a day in the program. Each of the district's two junior high schools was given six-tenths of a counselor's time for chemical dependency work. Central office people were extremely cooperative in working out the budget. Approval would not have been possible had administration been unwilling to attempt to understand the problem which the schools faced. A school district must gain key administrative faith and support for a program of this type.

In the spring of 1977, program sponsors presented to the board a budget proposal for the 1977-78 school year. The board agreed to an increase of staffing over the previous year. This increased total counseling services at the high school to one full time and one six-tenths time and provided a counselor full time at each junior high school. This sum also provided funding for the Johnson Institute program for counseling and staff training for the school year. The budget remained the same for the 1978-79 school year.

Only time will tell whether the Board of Education will continue to budget the program. But those who are responsible for the program believe that not only is there more success in getting people into treatment, but that there is also an intangible and unmeasurable attitude change occuring. This change seems to be developing not only with students, but also with faculty, parents, and community. There is a subdued acceptance of the need for a program. There is a new willingness to face the words *chemical dependency* without panic.

The faculty is now willing to attend workshops, knowing that they are not being threatened individually. This is also true of the administration and the Board of Education. Members of the community are willing to make public commitments to sobriety and to aid the program. The change is an attitudinal change, resulting from the program in its total being, not from one person or from one part. Because of this attitude of acceptance and willingness to become a part of the program on the part of the faculty, because of the community acceptance, and because of the superintendent's and assistant superintendent's willingness to participate, the Board of Education finds credibility and is thus willing to provide funds. A great amount of money is not necessary to begin a program. Training and awareness come first. With awareness, staffing will become a reality. Most teachers who know of problems will try to help with them. The budget need not be either monumental or the first problem.

After suffering all the frustrations which arose in attempting to gain budgeting, the organizers are convinced that submitting facts and figures about a problem and expecting people to accept them simply will not work. But boards and administrators can be lured into backing a program if some of them are willing to examine their own use and abuse. In-service training and shared personal convictions must work together to create a climate of concern and trust, and that concern and trust must exist before budgeting will be successful.

Chapter Five

The District and the Johnson Institute

Essential to formulation of the Wayzata School District policy on chemical dependency was the district's relationship with the Johnson Institute, an extremely fortunate relationship, since the Institute offers one of the most effective programs available anywhere. Founded to provide assistance to businesses and to families suffering from the effects of chemical abuse, the Institute had become interested in the problems affecting school districts at about the same time that some faculty members at Wayzata began to recognize the destructive role chemical abuse was playing in the lives of many students. Wayzata turned to the Institute for advice, and, in turn, Institute personnel offered scholarships for summer training for three members of the high school staff. That summer training in 1975 was an early and important step in the development of the school program.

Since that initial experience, a substantial number of

teachers and staff have participated in one or another of
the workshops available at the Institute. All secondary
school counselors have attended, most of the district's
principals have participated, teachers from a variety of
disciplines have attended, and all at district expense. Dr.
Manning has often said that one of his goals was to have
every teacher in the senior high school experience some
kind of training by 1985, although he admits that this will
be a difficult goal to achieve.

Teachers go to workshops for many reasons. For
example, some choose to participate for personal growth.
Others have had a number of students who were harmfully involved. Still others want to be able to recognize
symptoms early and to offer meaningful support to the
student who wants and needs it. Occasionally the subject
matter in a class such as health or some form of science is
related to chemical use. Administrators may select teachers for workshops in order to provide key people at
various points in the district to act as informal resource
persons. Conversations in lounges and over lunch are
excellent opportunities to share feelings, attitudes, and
basic information. These conversations are also, unfortunately, just as good opportunities for sharing misinforma-
tion. But experienced people who are present can calm
fears or correct wrong impressions.

Before they are enrolled, participants at workshops
agree to two major points. They are willing to support the
program and they are willing to take a look at themselves.

The first point, willingness to support the program, is a
vital one. Those who attended a workshop do not
necessarily become involved until they are comfortable.
They are not forced to participate at a level for which they
are not ready. However, they must agree that they will

support the goals of the program. They will not act as roadblocks or in any other way interfere with the progress of activities.

The second point, willingness to take a look at themselves, is a logical one. The intent of the workshop is to encourage self-study, not necessarily in the area of chemical use — that will be automatic — but in areas such as feelings, attitudes, and needs. Basic to the activities of the group is the need to get in touch with one's feelings and to improve positive self-concepts. If an individual does not choose to cooperate with this intent, there is no reason for that individual to become part of the group.

Teachers from Wayzata have participated in three or four types of workshops. The most complete workshop is a three-week program. During that period, participants work in two areas of activity. The first concentrates on skill development. Such skills as the abilities to recognize problems and evaluate needs, to understand verbal and non-verbal behavior, and to give feedback are valuable for everyone, but they are especially important to those who are concerned with chemical abuse. The all-important skill of *listening* is part of the study. Special attention goes to facilitating interventions.

In addition to skill development, participants give attention to other topics, some of which relate to facets of dependency such as the disease concept, the delusionary memory systems, chemical dependency among women, family involvement, and the state called "dry drunk." Participants examine various methods of approaching chemical abuse. Meaningful intervention, pharmacology, and group techniques are subject for study and discussion, as are A.A., Alanon, and Alateen.

As part of the three-week workshop, participants spend

a week in an internship at a treatment facility. Minneapolis, St. Paul, and the surrounding areas have several excellent treatment centers of various types. Most are designed to treat individuals of all ages, although one or the other works specifically with young people. A week at one of these centers is a concentrated look at needs and at ways to meet those needs.

A two-week workshop is also offered. Discussion and study materials cover virtually the same skill and concept areas as those offered in the three-week program. The major difference is that this program does not include an internship.

A much shorter offering is a one-week workshop, a short awareness activity meant to help people become aware of the disease of chemical dependency, the delusionary systems, and treatment. Participants in this group also examine problems of family illness.

A fourth workshop, one aimed specifically at family illness, is also available at the Johnson Institute. Subjects discussed at this workshop deal with identifying facets of dependency — illness of a spouse, of children, family systems, sexuality — or with approaches for dealing with dependency — A.A., Alanon, and Alateen; self-awareness and personal growth; and meaningful intervention and family counseling.

Counseling of those who are harmfully involved with chemicals is intensely personal. Those who are involved in developing a school program will want to take advantage of opportunities for special training in the field. Unfortunately, the most strenuous academic preparation for regular school counseling probably does not do much more than touch on the particular skills required for work with those who are harmfully involved with chemicals.

An effective program will begin with a solid training program for as many leaders as possible. An organization such as the Johnson Institute has immeasurable value in establishing a solid core of well-trained personnel.

Chapter Six

The Program for Faculty and Staff

"Do you really have the right to intrude in the personal life and habits of a faculty member?"

After four years of a program that is supposed to bring about awareness, concern, and acceptance of chemical dependency as a disease, this question always comes as a shock to those who are most deeply involved. However, the question continues to arise and it will arise on occasion in the thinking of even the most dedicated advocate of the program.

It is appropriate that the question should arise again and again. In a society which places value on the rights of individuals, a society which is concerned with invasion of privacy, a society which passes laws and performs other efforts for insuring the protection of individual rights, concerned people will continue to ask themselves the question. They will continue to do everything they can to assure themselves that no unnecessary intrusion into the personal lives of others will occur. For people working within the program, the question is a reminder that they must be constantly alert. They must never become so zealous in their advocacy that they overstep the bounds of personal rights.

However, those who work within the program know that the question of involvement in the personal lives of faculty members often comes from feelings less worthy than respect for the rights of others. In many cases the question arises from indifference or disinterest; in other instances it is prompted by fear.

Indifference and disinterest are common reasons for questioning the school's right to intrude in the personal lives of its faculty. People who have not yet accepted the disease concept of chemical dependency or developed concern for their co-workers may raise the question — if they are pressed to consider the matter at all — simply because they feel that the whole thing is not worth the time and effort being expended. These people feel detached from the problem. They have closed their eyes to the effects of harmful involvement with chemicals, and feel confident that the abuse of chemicals will never touch them anyway. That confidence is probably false, but it is a comforting one.

Another cause for raising the question of the school's right is fear. Individuals who prefer not to examine their own use will often speak most ardently against any facet of the program, or they may resist in some other way which reflects their fear. A philosophy which encourages — indeed demands — that individuals examine their own use is often a serious threat. People who feel threatened may be righteous and indignant about "witch hunts" and angrily demand that their rights "be respected."

The answer to the question of intrusion certainly does not come easily. Anyone beginning a program designed to treat harmful involvement among faculty members will discover that an answer reached at one point in time may need to be affirmed again and again. Most members of a society framed by principles of individual rights will need to remind themselves over and over that there are times when giving help to one person necessarily means involving another person — even when that other person is unwilling to be approached. Some would call an approach to a person unwilling to be approached an "intrusion."

But in the case of secondary and primary school teachers — along with many other classes of persons — it would seem that the nature of their relationship to the students would preclude calling such an involvement, however unwanted, an intrusion.

In order for a program to be successful, the answer to the question, "Do you really have the right to be involved in the personal life and habits of a faculty member?" must be an unhesitating "Yes." However, for the three groups just described, reaching that agreement may be a difficult thing.

The first group, organizers of the program and those most directly involved, will have little difficulty reaching agreement. For these people, however, there may still be moments of doubt. Faced with the necessity of acting on their conviction that a fellow worker who is harmfully involved needs intervention and treatment, even the most dedicated person must occasionally feel hesitant. It is no small matter to take action, to risk friendship and good feeling. Only a person who believes his judgments are always perfect can escape doubt, and people trained in work with chemical dependency know the dangers of believing in their own perfection. Intellectually, however, this group knows that involvement is necessary. This belief will help overcome occasional doubt.

The second group, those who are indifferent or disinterested, are harder to convince. For them an answer of yes to the question of involvement will be much more difficult. These people are immersed in their own affairs, convinced that they already have enough to do. They resist any change in their routine and consider such events as in-service programs to be annoying interruptions in their time. Indifferent people, however, are not impossible to reach — just hard. Organizers of programs will have to do a fair amount of firm insisting on the importance of their ideas, but they can eventually overcome both indifference and disinterest if they provide enough real education on the subject.

The group most difficult to bring to agreement on the question will be those who answer no out of fear. Their negative response to the importance of a program designed to help those who are harmfully involved will be a response generated by feeling, not by reason. And fear is a strong feeling. It is also a great defense. For many who — for reasons they may not even be able to put into words for themselves — resist a program for chemically dependent individuals, the feeling may be almost overpowering. Certainly strong fear resists reason. Fearful people may say, "I don't care what your reasons are, I just don't like it!"

They may even be able to say, "I don't care what your reasons are, I'm afraid of it," and explain that fear on various grounds: "I'm afraid we're getting into areas we're not trained to handle," or "I'm afraid that once they get started with this program, they'll be interfering with all of our lives."

These people recognize fear, even voice fear, but they do not really acknowledge fear's source — their reluctance to examine their own use of alcohol.

Overcoming the resistance this group offers to the question of involvement in personal lives of faculty is very difficult. Organizers and supporters of new programs must listen carefully to the spoken fears. They must explain that the real business of the school cannot go on if students and faculty are not functioning well and are suffering from chemical abuse. They must explain that training is available and that staff people will have plenty of assistance from trained personnel. They must explain that in no way will any program become a witch hunt with administrative big brothers listing the number of parties each person attends. They must, in every possible way, provide reassurance that fear is normal however unnecessary, and that the real motivation behind any school program dealing with dependency is concern.

Concern must be the key. All of the three groups — the dedicated, the indifferent, and the fearful — will eventually agree to the right of involvement if they understand that the need is based on genuine concern. And the program can become successful only if it is based on sincere caring and concern.

A school faculty is a caring group. Those who choose to work with young people enjoy personal contacts. Teachers and other school staff members learn to be constantly alert to the needs of others. Successful classroom experiences grow from successful human relations. They depend on give-and-take between teacher and student, on sensitive awareness of reactions. The school with a successful academic program will be a school with a staff of people who have experience in dealing with others and who genuinely care about their relationships with others. This group of people will respond to the program which develops an atmosphere of trust and a climate of concern.

It is unfortunate that harmful involvement with chemicals is a disease which, unlike most other diseases, leads to alienation. It is still regarded by some as a moral problem. Most individuals have experienced at some time the warm and loving drawing together which occurs within a family when one member suffers from a serious illness. Warmth and concern extend into the community and neighbors step in to provide hot dishes, to do yard work, to paint houses, or to put on benefit dinners or dances. Good feeling thrives and a warm sensation of worth supports both the sufferer and the family.

Chemical dependency, however, does not have this effect. Instead of warm and loving drawing together, alienation and rejection characterize reactions to this disease. Moreover, alienation extends beyond the family and into the community. The sufferer is rejected everywhere and finds in this rejection further reason to turn to the abuse of chemicals.

Just as alcoholism tends to alienate family members, it also serves as an alienating force within a school faculty. Through education, family members may eventually be helped to change their feelings of rejection to acceptance and support. In the same way, fellow faculty members must be helped to change their feelings. When staff members are educated about the disease concept of dependency, when they can at least recognize the cause of the alienation which develops when a fellow worker is harmfully involved with chemicals, and when they can begin to deal with that alienation, their concern for other people can function. Concern, acceptance, support — these positive relationships can begin to replace negative attitudes.

Concern, however, has to be channeled into significant activity. It must not be allowed to deteriorate into passive acceptance or misguided compensation for ineffective work. A concerned faculty, guided by trained personnel in in-service programs, can come to recognize the signs which suggest developing problems and can participate in early intervention. Early intervention provides the best kind of assistance for the individual who is harmfully involved with chemicals. Teachers and staff must come to know that not to be involved in this kind of assistance is enabling co-workers to continue abuse. Not to be involved may be hurrying the death of a friend or acquaintance.

Staff members need to learn to recognize the symptoms of harmful involvement.

Absenteeism is a symptom in many cases. Excessive absenteeism should always be questioned, and it can be one of the prime indicators of harmful involvement with chemicals. This is true, of course, of students; it is also true of faculty.

Bizarre behavior of one kind or another is a second indication of harmful involvement. Bizarre behavior can take many directions. There are some kinds, however, which are fairly common. Temper tantrums are one form. Explosions of temper for reasons which seem fairly insignificant to observers should alert co-workers. Another form of bizarre behavior may be the use of unusually violent or obscene language in inappropriate circumstances. Individuals who are using chemicals to a harmful degree may be irritable, hard to get along with. They may be extremely inflexible to such a degree that they are difficult to work with in any kind of team situation. In addition advanced abuse may cause blackouts which result in memory loss. Most people forget things occasionally, but the memory losses of a dependent person are often noticeable.

As a result of bizarre behavior, individuals who are using chemicals heavily will often alienate other staff members. It is not unusual for these individuals to withdraw completely from social relationships with fellow faculty members, even from those fairly minor social relationships which occur within a common office area during the regular school day.

Evidence of harmful involvement may also include a general slowing down of productivity. A teacher may continue to teach with apparent mastery. However, close examination will reveal that this teacher continues to follow the same lesson plans he or she has used for several years. Teachers who are abusing resist changes in the curriculum which will force them into developing new plans. This characteristic is not obvious, since the reluctance to change is often disguised as a desire to continue to do what one does best.

Fellow teachers will only recognize this characteristic if they examine how often they themselves are called upon to prepare new lesson plans and to react to new curriculum demands. Teachers who thrive on variety and enjoy the challenge of new subject matter will be slow to recognize the reluctance to change which is typical of the dependent person.

More obvious, but often simply passed over as idiosyncracy, is the fact that the dependent individual may fall into a pattern of coming late to his job and of leaving early at the end of the day. Many times persons who are harmfully involved will have learned to plead other responsibilities, other regular activities, which make it necessary for them to leave early and which explain the fact that they may often miss department meetings or other activities which are part of the normal routine of the school.

Another obvious indication of harmful involvement is the physical evidence which those who work closely together will notice. Blood-shot eyes are a stereotypical sign, of course. Generally speaking, however, stereotypes develop from truths. Breath fresheners certainly do their job, but constant use of these products is suspect. Another slightly more subtle indication is the whole question of grooming. A usually smart dresser may gradually become less concerned with the fine points of dress and take to wearing the same outfits over and over, although co-workers know that he or she has an extensive wardrobe.

All of these symptoms sound fairly simple. Difficulty in diagnosing harmful involvement derives from the fact that symptoms may exist in varying degrees or in varying combinations. By no means do all people display all symptoms.

A further complication in diagnosis arises from a quite opposite form of behavior. Experienced people recognize this pattern and call it CYA, a somewhat more socially acceptable reference to an expression which means "Cover your rear." This behavior is an attempt to avoid the alienation which usually characterizes harmful involve-ment. This individual attempts to endear himself or herself to administration and peers. Super-efficiency is the key. The goal apparently is to become the perfect employee.

These people are always out and about, coming in early in the morning, operating with great efficiency. They do favors. They are highly visible in their activities. These people take on a father- or mother-like role with students. They do the little mechanical things most teachers dislike doing, and they do them without complaint. Unfortunately, however, efficiency does not carry over to the major area of responsibility. Productivity in that area slows down, just as it does for others who are harmfully involved. That slow-down may be even more significant in this case because of the preoccupation with efficiency and with details.

The defense which these individuals raise for themselves is a subtle one. They trap their co-workers into feeling sorry for them. Fellow teachers unconsciously try to protect these people. No one wants to feel guilty about suggesting that problems exist. Everyone is drawn into denying the illness. Everyone is drawn into participating in the destruction of a healthy, productive individual.

When faced with the suggestion of a problem, this individual and any other individual who is harmfully involved will almost surely deny that any problem exists at all. Those who are dependent may continue to deny the problem even when faced with overwhelming evidence from family and friends.

When indications of harmful involvement appear to fellow staff people, the situation will have reached a point beyond which danger lies. Family and friends will already be aware of problems. Many people will have evidence of harmful involvement, but because they dislike gossip or because they respect their acquaintances' right to privacy, they will not have compared notes. School people should

overcome this reticence and learn when to check their
observations with one another to determine whether
others share their concern.

The difficult task before those who see harmful involvement developing is the task of taking action. For most
Americans raised in an atmosphere of concern for others,
the obvious action is to protect these individuals from
their own symptoms.

If they don't want to teach new classes, let them teach
the ones they want to teach, we say. So we willingly take
on the new classes. If we know what makes them angry,
we'll just avoid those things. So we tip-toe around tender
subjects to keep peace at any cost. If they don't want to
come to department meetings, we write decisions down,
ditto them off, and pass them along. If the victims of
dependency forget earlier discussions and want to rehash
problems already solved, we go along. And if the inflexi-
bility leads to endless repetition of grievances, we listen
and nod. For the sake of the students we have to keep
things smooth, we say. There are any number of reasons
why it is not right to stir up trouble. Not the least of these
reasons is the fear of risking a friendship.

Better to risk losing a friendship, however, than to risk
the life of a friend. A concerned faculty that has accepted
the disease concept of dependency will know that if some
kind of intervention does not occur, the person who is
abusing with chemicals may be shortening his or her life.

What do we do? Whatever is done, whether it be
concerned one-to-one talk or a planned intervention, is
better than doing nothing. Doing *something* forces the
abuser to take a look at his or her use. We must take some
action.

Taking action probably means intervention. Intervention, in a very special sense of the word, is used in the context of a program dealing with chemical dependency. One-to-one talks may have some value, but a serious case of harmful involvement probably requires more concentrated action. Intervention in this sense refers to a planned and carefully organized confrontation between an individual who is harmfully involved with chemicals and his or her friends and acquaintances who cooperate in their efforts to force that individual to recognize his or her illness and examine its cause. Intervention as used in the Wayzata school system follows the plan developed by the Johnson Institute. Training sessions held at the Institute include training in the use of this process.

Intervention must begin with the accumulation of data. This is the kind of activity which most people dislike, since it carries the suggestion of spying. In practice, however, any person closely involved with an individual who is abusing with chemicals usually has some pretty clear evidence of symptoms right at hand. It is not necessary to pry or sneak to develop data. Several friends or co-workers brought together with each contributing one suggestion of a symptom will find that they have among them enough data to convince themselves first of all that intervention is necessary.

One concerned person must set the process going. With the help of a counselor, an individual trained in handling interventions, this concerned person can call together a group of co-workers and friends of the one about whom they are concerned. Together, these people examine their experiences. In most cases each person is able to contribute some piece of data which suggests harmful involvement. If these pieces fit together to form a picture of growing dependency, the group will also see a picture of real pain for a sufferer and a family. Recognizing this pain motivates the group to continue the process.

The next step should be a training session for the intervention group. One important subject of this training session must be the assurance that the people involved are willing to take a risk. The risk may mean the loss of a friendship. If one of the interested persons is the spouse of the individual under consideration, the risk to that person is tremendous.

Each of the members of the group must examine the picture the data reveals. Each one must weigh the pain of the victim against the risks involved. Each one must reaffirm his belief in the progressive nature of dependency and the fact that progressive dependency may lead to premature death. Usually each individual in the group feels the support which is necessary to motivate him or her to present data and to take part in the intervention.

The third step, a final group meeting before the intervention, rehearses the entire process. At this meeting some of the group may be eliminated. If the data some individuals have to offer is purely repetitious for no good purpose, these individuals should not be involved in the intervention.

As a major part of this final meeting, all alternatives for action beyond the intervention should be reviewed. There should be a clear understanding of what treatment possibilities will be offered, as well as an understanding of what the results will be if the alternatives are not acceptable — if treatment is refused.

It is important to note here that the boss or supervisor of the subject of the intervention should definitely be part of the intervention group. People who have become harmfully involved with chemicals will suffer the loss of family, of a spouse, and of friends more readily than they will suffer the loss of the job. The insistence that it is necessary to maintain that job will be an important part of any resistance to treatment. For this reason, a successful school program will be founded on the assumption that it is vital to assure faculty and staff that accepting treatment for dependency will not endanger their jobs. Policy may state that failure to recognize a need and accept some form of treatment may lead to the loss of a job, but going into treatment should not be penalized and this must be clearly stated.

Job performance will inevitably suffer if an individual is harmfully involved with chemicals. Data on that job performance is an extremely significant part of the intervention process. That data, however, should be used as an encouragement to accept treatment, not as a threat. The harmfully involved individual must be assured that he has the capacity to do his work well and that treatment is necessary to allow him to work at the level of his ability.

The first course of action of the intervention group should be to encourage the ill person to enter a hospital or treatment center, just as he would do if he were suffering from any other disease. This inpatient handling of the illness is by far the most productive. It will most rapidly restore an individual to top performance on the job and to full participation in his activities outside the job.

A second course of action is outpatient treatment. This kind of treatment is usually held after working hours and includes nightly and weekend activities in a therapeutic setting, either a hospital or a treatment center. The program should involve both patient and family. It should be an acceptable action if the first goal of inpatient care is adamantly rejected. This program will necessarily require a longer period of time before progress can be observed.

A third option for the individual is to join Alcoholics Anonymous. A.A. is highly successful. It does, however, require a longer period of time to produce observable progress. Membership in an A.A. group is most successful when it parallels or follows either inpatient or outpatient treatment. Active membership in an A.A. group should, however, be a viable alternative for the dependent person.

Unfortunately, though, there will be instances in which an intervention meets a stone wall of resistance to any form of treatment. Since this does occasionally occur, the group should agree, before the intervention takes place, on just what their united reaction will be if the subject of the intervention refuses any treatment and insists that he can — and will — simply stop drinking. The response to this insistence will have to be a pre-determined answer to the question, "What if you use again?"

One answer might come from a spouse. "If you drink once more and do not or will not enter treatment, we are through."

Another possible answer might come from the boss, "If you drink once more and do not or will not enter treatment, you will be fired."

Both these answers are "Hard Love" statements. These individuals love the ill person enough to take the risk of losing that person as a spouse or as an employee. This loss is the alternative to letting the dependent person continue abusing. The Hard Love position may, in cases of adamant resistance to treatment, be the only position those who really care can take.

This final meeting of the intervention group must

satisfy each member of the group. All of those involved in this rehearsal must believe that the individual about whom they are concerned will be offered as much support and as much care as it is within the power of the school system to provide. This belief must include assurance that every possible care will be taken to maintain the income and protect the job of the victim of the disease. The group must be united in this belief. A united group, believing in the desire of the school to provide for one of their co-workers, will be able to transmit that belief to their suffering friend. Supporting one another in their belief and in their caring, they should be able to create a caring atmosphere to ease the distress of the ill person, the focus of their concern.

When the intervention group is satisfied that they have sufficient data to reveal harmful involvement with chemicals, the time has come to present that data. An appointment is set up, the group gathers, and the confrontation begins. One by one, the members of the group present to the dependent their data, their pieces of the picture of pain and suffering.

Wife: "On October 24, 27, November 3, 11, and 14, you came home drunk."

"On November 11 you received a ticket for drunken driving."

"On our anniversary last year you were so drunk I had to drive home."

"You used to share our budget with me. You no longer leave money for food, and we are going into debt. You always have money for liquor."

"You ran into the garage door when you came home on November 14."

Friend: "You told me you weren't drinking, but you

had drinks at noon with me on three occasions: August 15, September 20, and September 26."

"You forgot a business appointment with me on November 3."

Boss: "On October 20 you had liquor on your breath when we met with a customer. You were very negative in this meeting."

"You have missed work six days in the last three weeks for a variety of illnesses."

"You have three reports that were due a week ago that are still not in."

Daughter; "You've promised me three times that you would visit my school and you've forgotten all three times."

When concerned persons gather together there will be many more examples of behavior that is not acceptable and which comes from the individual's abuse of chemicals.

Facts about an individual's behavior must be presented as facts — just that. There should be no judgment in the presentation. This group is not involved in any moral examination of behavior. The data should, as much as possible, combine to create the picture which others have discerned, a picture of an individual who has lost his productiveness, who is suffering, who is abusing with chemicals, but who is worth saving and who can once again become a productive person.

There is, of course, a great deal of uneasiness and real distress related to intervention, not only for the individual being confronted but also for those who confront him. Many hours of sleep will have been lost, many meals left uneaten, and much time spent in agonizing indecision before the confrontation finally occurs. Added to the risk of losing spouse or friend is the fact that, faced with an occasion when what they do or say will have deep and lasting effect on a fellow human being, most people become unsure. They feel humble and afraid and long for the security of disinterest. "How did I ever let myself be drawn into this?" they may lament. Here again, genuine concern will be the key, and the combined awareness of the group offers support.

Intervention usually is successful to some degree, although sometimes the success is only the beginning of a long and difficult period of tentative decisions and frequent back-sliding. The major purpose, the desire to force an individual to examine his or her abuse with chemicals, is almost always accomplished. The results of that examination, however, may take some time to develop. Intervention normally leads to professional help of one kind or another or to some kind of help outside the school itself. Either inpatient or outpatient treatment brings the patient into the care of professionals. If the alternative the individual chooses is A.A., the experience is also outside the school.

To hope for immediate change is naive; to expect some miracle cure is totally unrealistic. There are, however, some things left to do: to wait, to offer support, and to continue to care.

Chapter Seven

The Program for Students

Tremendous things go on in high schools. Visitors walking through a school in session cannot help but be impressed by the varied activities in classrooms and other meeting places. In the controlled, near-quiet of a class hour, a visitor moving through the halls may hear bits of lectures on ancient history, the sound track of a film presentation on circulatory systems, the purposeful clack of typewriters competing against time in a drill, or the rhythmic bounce of basketballs. Student stores, language resource centers, computer centers, and a well-used library accentuate the possibilities open to today's students. After-school-hours are just as busy. Athletic programs for boys and girls sprawl from gymnasiums and wrestling rooms into hallways and the out-of-doors. Trophy cases, bulletin boards, music groups, yearbooks, and dramatic performances of all kinds attest to the willingness of a large percentage of high school students to put time and almost unbelievable energy into both studies and extra-curricular activities.

Against the clear, bright picture of learning and productivity, the blurred, dark image of youngsters who are harmfully involved with chemicals is a sorry contrast. And youngsters suffering from pains inflicted by a family torn by the effects of chemical abuse in parent or sibling also often stand alone. Unhappy, frustrated in the attempt to fit a pattern their peers find natural, these young persons have increasingly limited success and increasing difficulty just keeping up with themselves. Because these youngsters do not fit the expectations of the schools and their peers, they may be disciplined, scoffed at, or — perhaps worse — ignored. The endless flow of activity simply moves around them.

Frequently, however, something happens which focuses attention on those troubled young people. Sometimes the focus may be kindly, sometimes cruel. Occasionally the attention will be helpful; quite often it only adds to the problem.

Symptoms which suggest harmful involvement may be difficult to identify. A young person may suddenly be ill, vomiting in the back corner of a classroom. In the flurry of cleaning up and dealing with a disrupted class, a teacher has to ask himself whether the student may be abusing with chemicals or whether he is sick from other causes. If a student frequently falls asleep in class, a concerned teacher must determine whether that student is abusing with chemicals, expressing boredom in a fairly positive manner, or simply losing sleep at more appropriate times.

Staff people in a high school see all too many students experiencing real difficulty with basic skills in writing and apparently having trouble reading. Again, only careful examination will determine whether the trouble can be traced to a real lack of skills or whether the appearance of such a lack stems from inertia or lethargy caused by chemical abuse. Frequent absenteeism is another possible indication of trouble, but one to which it is even more difficult to assign a cause. The student who misses a number of classes remains almost a stranger to teachers who have many students to work with.

A good chemical dependency program in a high school accepts the fact that faculty and staff members cannot always recognize harmful involvement with chemicals. All classroom teachers cannot be experts in diagnosis and they will distrust and resist a program which assumes that they will be. Successful programs which have begun at the top administrative level and moved through in-service activities for teachers to a well-structured plan for students still cannot hope to educate all teachers to deal with the symptoms of harmful involvement. Such programs should establish two goals for teachers' participation:

1) Educate teachers to the value of and the need for a school program.
2) Provide channels for teachers to refer students who appear to be in trouble to staff specialists who will be able to evaluate the whole picture.

The first goal, education of teachers as to value and need, requires reiteration of some commonly accepted ideas.

First, 97% of all high school students use chemicals somewhere along a line that begins with experimentation and ends with abuse. This figure is our best possible estimate, and it is based on a great deal of evidence. Students who have learned to trust staff people and who recognize the seriousness of the problem indicate that it is almost impossible to find any function at which there is no use of chemicals. Experimentation may be as simple as tasting wine at a family dinner or drinking half a can of beer at a party. Abuse begins when the individual begins to experience pain as a result of his use.

A second significant figure to emphasize is that 90% of the chemicals used is alcohol. Marijuana or pot is a common companion to alcohol. When professional people at the Johnson Institute developed a chart, rating addicting qualities of various substances, they ranked pot above nicotine and caffeine but well below ethyl alcohol. The effects of marijuana are still not clear. However, parents who have been dismayed by the thought of pot, both because of possible physical effects and because of possible prosecution for possession, are less concerned about alcohol. Alcohol is the choice of most adults looking for mood-altering effects; it is also the choice of most students.

A third important consideration is that studies show that, like the adult population, 12-15% of students who use are on the way to dependency. In this country, one out of every seven people who use will become dependent. The program at Wayzata recognizes that it is almost impossible to prevent students' use of chemicals. The program is, instead, aimed at educating students and staff about the consequences of use so that early recognition of abuse can moderate the harmful effects.

When teachers really become aware of these consequences, when they can look at a classroom and realize that at least four students out of their own favorite classes of about twenty-eight face the probability of dependency, and when those figures apply to real people about whom they have come to care a great deal, then those teachers will understand the value of a program aimed at recognizing trouble and offering a helping hand.

In schools this becomes more acceptable when faculties recognize that the goal of a school program is not to decide whether anyone — students, faculty members, or parents — is dependent. Rather the goals are to recognize symptoms of harmful involvement, to intervene in such a way as to make it possible for the sufferer to see the effects of this involvement, and to provide opportunity and support for his or her efforts to eliminate chemical abuse.

Again, however, a word of caution is necessary. This education of faculty must begin with the idea that it is impossible just to fix up students. An effective program is based on the assumption that faculty and administration will first have looked at their own use. A program's effectiveness is measured by the extent to which faculty and students will continue to examine their use and will continue to grow in understanding and concern.

A program which concentrates only on students, Wayzata's organizers found, will simply be bottlenecked. Faculties may feel good in such a one-sided program. There is some pleasure in the feeling that one is acting to improve someone else, but smug altruism is only temporarily satisfying. Genuine effectiveness derives from willingness on the part of principals, counselors, and teachers to examine their own use. The possibility of success depends on this self-examination and the self-knowledge which results. Incidentally, this self-examination is valuable even to those faculty members whose use of chemicals is limited to a glass of wine at Thanksgiving and Christmas. The understanding of self which such a process of self-examination encourages and the increased awareness of human feelings, desires, and needs which result are pluses for the whole system. When an atmosphere of openness and acceptance exists, everyone profits.

In such an atmosphere, perceptive teachers may observe in students symptoms which suggest harmful involvement. Such things as fluctuation of mood, varying reliability or productivity, and frequent absenteesim combine with physical symptoms to elicit concern from a teacher.

An effective program must provide an easy referral process; in addition the process must be non-threatening. Normal demands on a teacher's time are often heavy. A referral system which is time-consuming or complicated will not be welcomed and may not be used. All teachers will want to feel free to alert counselors to possible problems without threatening their relationships with students. Teacher-student relationships are often fragile, particularly in the instance of troubled students, and trust is often difficult to achieve.

Although a teacher may not see a referral to a chemical dependency counselor as a breach of trust — indeed, he may see it as an expression of his deepest concern — the student may have quite a different view. Knowing this, teachers may be reluctant to make referrals unless they are assured of confidentiality. For these reasons Wayzata's referral system is very simple. A name on a slip of paper handed to the chemical dependency staff will suffice. In addition, the official policy states: "Referral sources will remain confidential until after initial contact is made with the student and parent or guardian."

Referrals may come from sources other than teachers. Parents may refer their youngsters. School counselors and administrators may act as referral sources within the school. Occasionally, social workers, law enforcement personnel, or an officer of the court may use the school program. On a less official level, but equally effective and respected, are referrals from the peer group of friends or concerned fellow-students.

Some of the referrals to the program at Wayzata arise from the students themselves and some of their approaches to the program are concerned not with student use but with use by some member of a student's family. One of the important functions of the program is its service to young people who are suffering because a parent, grandparent, or sibling is abusing with chemicals. For many of these young people, the knowledge that others must deal with family abuse is a tremendous boost to self-esteem.

At Wayzata one interesting method of contacting students is through classroom visits. At the request of individual teachers, chemical dependency counselors and a few students who have participated in support groups come into classes for an hour or two to describe the program and to respond to students' questions about it. Interest is high. Many students wonder, "What goes on in group?" This is an extremely valuable communication since it offers an assurance from peers which is essential for many young people.

Another kind of referral is that which develops through other programs available at Wayzata. The high school offers several special services for young people who are not achieving academically the level they could reach. Teachers often know that students are not working as well as they are able to do. This may be true at all levels of ability. Class discussions and one-to-one relationships between teachers and students often reveal degrees of perception and understanding which test scores or written assignments do not substantiate. If the under-achievement is fairly consistent, teachers at Wayzata refer these students to resource specialists for evaluation. Occasionally the evaluation which begins with a focus on academic weakness will reveal causes related to chemical abuse by the student or by some family member.

Once a referral is made, the procedure for handling it follows a routine carefully established by school policy. The chemical dependency counselor will contact the student for an initial interview. Using experiences with the program and knowledge of students and their needs, the counselor can conduct one or more interviews to determine whether the student is harmfully involved with chemicals or whether the problems which led to referral derive from another source. The keynote of these interviews is concern. A successful chemical dependency counselor quickly acquires a reputation for caring, and that reputation travels rapidly through the student population. If the counselor cares and students believe he or she is fair and understanding, word gets around. And as the word gets around, taking a risk with the counselor — trusting — becomes easier.

Counselors develop lists of questions which they find useful in initial interviews. *I'll Quit Tomorrow* by Vernon Johnson, founder of the Johnson Institute, contains sample interviews covering general biographical information as well as information related to chemical use. Questionnaires of this kind based on school-related activities are useful and revealing. School chemical dependency counselors usually have to be particularly perceptive, however. Even students who trust the counselor have a long habit of reticence. Only a genuine atmosphere of concern combined with skill and care can elicit the information which will help the counselor determine the appropriate direction to take with a student.

When the counselor has made such a determination of direction, he or she can recommend to the principal and to the student's regular school counselor a course of action for that student. This action might involve a commitment to several weeks in a school group program to acquire more knowledge of the harmful consequences of chemical use or to receive further evaluation within the group. The recommended action may suggest inpatient treatment or outpatient treatment. These two recommendations usually include intervention procedures similar to those used with faculty members or family members. The chemical dependency counselor may determine that, for the individual he is working with, active participation in an A.A. group is the appropriate step. As sometimes happens, the counselor may decide that no real problem exists and that there is no need for immediate concern.

When the counselor has made a determination, he contacts the student's parents, expressing his concern over the student's situation and identifying the specific difficulties which the student is encountering. These difficulties, ranging from problems with attendance through poor grades to more dramatic episodes of insolence or insubordination, may be related to abuse with chemicals, he suggests, and backs up his suggestion with specific evidence. A counselor is careful not to make recommendations carelessly. He will have good data to support his opinions. The student's regular counselor also approaches the family to offer information about the student's situation as regards academic progress and to assure parents that they are warmly welcomed by parent support groups within the community.

Students, of course, often are extremely resistant to treatment or to any involvement with school group activity. Parents must be made aware of the student's need for help, as they should be made aware of the programs which the school offers to provide that help. If the student absolutely refuses treatment — when this is the course the counselor recommends — or if he or she refuses even to see the counselor at all, the parents or guardians are told that the next time the student comes to school drunk or high, he or she will be sent to a detoxification center. Minnesota state law permits this. Referral to a detoxification center has been necessary at Wayzata only once. Every effort is made to convince the student to appear for the interview. with the chemical dependency counselor and to cooperate with that counselor once a course of action is suggested. If this is not permissible by law in other states, courts can many times be convinced to issue official court orders to intervene on the student's behalf.

Occasionally a circumstance develops in which the student agrees to participate in the group program but insists that his parents should not be informed. Counselors and group members are familiar with this desire and recognize its importance. Experience shows, however, that with group support the student should be able to see the need for sharing his problems with parents or guardians. These students begin the program on their own initiative, but the expectation is that they must inform their parents after they have attended two group meetings.

For the student who agrees to go into treatment, either as a result of interviews with the chemical dependency counselor, confrontation with concerned persons, or after being involved in the school group program, there are many different types of treatment centers. Each has its own way of operating. In many centers, family involvement is taken for granted, and experience at Wayzata has convinced those who work with the program that family participation is necessary. Harmful involvement with chemicals on the part of one member is almost always an indication of suffering on the part of other members of the family and the goal of treatment should be to work toward improved health for them all.

Inpatient treatment in a hospital or treatment center for the student is, of course, the most concentrated form of treatment and, initially, probably the most productive. Inpatient programs involve the family in various ways, usually establishing a regular program which all of the family attends to receive counseling and support. All of these programs provide opportunities for families to interact in a safe setting, and such interaction allows parents and children to bring out and examine deeply-hidden feelings, thus providing the foundation for building good feeling and health.

Treatment can be conducted on an outpatient basis, and here again the family is often involved. Sessions are often conducted at a hospital or treatment center which provides the safe setting for examining problems, but the patient is not admitted to the hospital on a regular basis.

Another form of treatment is, of course, involvement in an organization such as Alcoholics Anonymous. This kind of organization also has provision for family members through the organization named Al-Anon. However, one drawback of using two separate self-help groups is that there is not the same emphasis on interaction between parents and students as under professional supervision.

All of these forms of treatment are acceptable options for treatment if the chemical dependency counselor and the school staff have determined that treatment is the appropriate approach. Individual cases logically invite individual handling. Generally speaking, however, two points are very clear: inpatient treatment leads to the most immediate results and family involvement is vital.

Support groups within the school are organized for several reasons. The first of these is to give support to students who come out of treatment and return to school. The return to school is a vital part of recovery. The group offers necessary understanding and concern to ease the real difficulty which the returning youngsters experience as they re-enter a familiar environment without the mood-altering chemicals which they had seen as one way of making that environment tolerable. They must meet again the friends with whom they had used chemicals and experience again the kinds of frustrations which they had formerly felt provided a reason for abuse.

Although treatment offers these youngsters an insight into their own experiences and starts them on a program toward understanding and coping with those experiences, it can only be a beginning. The strength to grow from that beginning comes in part from the support group. In addition, youngsters returning from treatment are role models for every student in school who is still using. They also are special role models for those who are struggling to remain sober. Within the support group, this role as model is affirmed and the unique value of every individual is emphasized. No student is pressed to become an ideal, pre-cast model of a sober student.

Another function of the support group is to provide help to those students who are still using and who have not yet taken a thorough look at themselves and the consequences of their chemical use. Often, the support group becomes the core of an intervention group which confronts a student and convinces the student that treatment is essential.

A third function of the support group is to offer help to students who come from families in which there is abuse. Even if these students do not use chemicals at all, they need help, because the illness of dependency attacks a whole family. Unlike the family in which a member is terminally ill and in which love and concern draw the whole family together, the family which suffers because one member is dependent is torn apart. The student who comes from such a family may often experience guilt because of a mistaken feeling of responsibility for the anger which develops in them. That student may devote tremendous energy and thought to attempts to reconcile family differences for which he or she is in no way responsible and which, indeed, are only symptoms of the sickness of the family. This student needs support from a group who can show that he or she is not responsible for the problems. The group can help the student understand what "enabling" is and how futile and even destructive enabling can be. Ideally, of course, the group can help the student from a suffering family lead that family into a program which may assist it. Practically, of course, this is not often the case. But the group can support the student and give that individual strength to live with the problem and to protect and improve his own self-esteem.

Support groups at Wayzata meet regularly, once a week for two hours. Obviously this is an interruption to normal school routine. Here again the acceptance of faculty is required. Those two hours represent missed classes and missed classes require cooperation. Students in group must take responsibility for making up the work they miss, but their efforts to do so should not meet unnecessary obstacles. Teachers have to accept the program and accept student participation without comment or judgment. But just as much, teachers should not be mistakenly solicitous and shrug off requests for make-up assignments. Students who are members of support groups need to take responsibility for themselves and the importance of their school work should not be discounted by indifference masked as kindheartedness.

It is, of course, extra work for teachers to supply make-up. Knowing, however, that a student will be gone regularly once a week on the same day, the teacher can make regular plans for assigning make-up. Moreover, the teacher has access to substantial assistance in handling any problems which may develop with that make-up, since the group is always ready to confront its members if difficulties arise in their carrying out responsibilities.

Teachers may be tempted to treat students in the group as special. And these students are special, of course. Young people who have recognized their harmful involvement with drugs and who are working to free themselves are certainly worthy of respect. Special respect, however, does not mean special privileges. The best consideration from faculty is the knowledge that these young people deserve the satisfaction of doing a tough job well. They deserve the little extra time from teachers; they have earned the right to be treated as responsible individuals.

One of the real blocks for the student for whom inpatient treatment is the recommended course of action has been the question of schooling. The desire to continue along a normal course of school life, to graduate with one's class, and to finish school on time from the student's point of view is a very reasonable desire. For young people in high school, a lost term seems like disaster, and at sixteen or seventeen, the prospect of remaining in high school for an additional time is horrifying.

One of the decisions which authorities at Wayzata made to ease going into treatment is the decision that students should receive full school credits for the time spent in treatment.

It is easy to justify this. The law requires special help in tutoring during this period, but the time for such help is limited. The intensity of the treatment program makes it impractical and undesireable to require hour for hour tutoring. However, a close look at the treatment program reveals an intensity of learning experiences which hour for hour the class room could hardly match.

The most obvious learning experience is certainly in the fields related to communications or English. The young person in treatment must communicate. He must learn to express himself, to be precise about his thoughts. He must learn to listen, to think critically, and to analyse the information he receives.

In much the same way, young people in treatment work with other areas which are part of school curriculums. Certainly they learn much about health. Treatment programs provide the physical activity of a physical education class. Sociology and psychology are part of the material, less formally, perhaps, than in social studies class but certainly more intensively. Recreational and therapeutic periods of treatment offer opportunity for creativity in arts and crafts.

Twenty-four-hour-a-day residence in a center designed

to keep individuals productively involved in self-examination and growing in self-esteem is a learning experience worthy of credit. Individuals will ask, of course, whether this kind of learning experience is the equivalent of academic work. Comparing credits awarded to growth in communications and self-esteem to credits given for mathematics, grammar, French, or typing does reveal some obvious differences.

However, the kind of concentrated learning experience involved in inpatient treatment usually lasts only about six weeks and provides the student with increased confidence and a feeling of purpose with which to tackle the skill courses and do the makeup work that is necessary to fill gaps in skills. The significant idea to note is that the student should not be penalized for time spent in treatment to the extent that he loses a large block of credits. He will, of course, expect to do individual work or to repeat courses which require skill development.

Since the program began in 1975 through June 1, 1981, approximately 362 students have gone into treatment. Most of them have returned to school. Virtually all have reached their senior year, and many have graduated, although for some of them the prospect had been dim. Although the life of the program is still too short to be the basis for definitive studies, current figures show that 77% of those students remain free of chemical use. Of the remaining 23%, many do experience relapses, but again, experience indicates that these relapses are usually temporary. An educated guess by one of the program's organizers suggests a success rate of about 97%. The organizers of the program, however, feel confident that for almost all of these young people, involvement in the program has led to self-understanding and personal strength. It is important to stress that over this same length of time more than sixty parents and thirty-seven teachers or their spouses have also entered treatment centers as a direct result of this program.

Most teachers can come up with some pretty specific examples of success. Take, for example, one teacher's story of Jessie:

"When Jessie started tenth grade, she was a pretty girl with the shiny hair and straight teeth that are products of comfortable middle-class living. Probably her most attractive feature, though, was that kind of wide-eyed eagerness that tenth grade girls can never quite hide behind the facade of blase indifference they work so hard to cultivate. It was quite obvious that Jessie was half-scared and half-excited by the whole senior high world, and that fear and excitement were so strong that she and her friends often forgot that I could usually hear when they were talking before class about their weekend plans. I wasn't always happy about what I heard. The need to be part of the "in" group was obviously stronger than any good judgment the girls had ever had. The plans got pretty complicated.

'You tell your mother you're going to stay with me, and I'll tell mine we're going to Jane's. Then we can go to the party at Bill's. Joe'll drive. His mom and dad are out of town and he just got his license.'

"It wasn't long before the talk centered on keggers and pot, and it got easier and easier for the girls to skip class and roam the halls looking for Joe or Bill or some other kids to help the current party along.

"Jessie wasn't in my class during the winter trimester, but I had her again in the spring. By then she was taking two classes in our department, which probably meant that she had flunked one during the winter term. We weren't very far into the new unit when it was pretty obvious that Jessie was having trouble getting to class. It was the last hour of the day, and that's always hard to make. I talked to her about her absences, and I finally called her mother. I had a little trouble reaching the mother, because she has a pretty responsible job and is out of the office quite a bit. But I did finally get through and she said she'd do what she could, although she didn't sound too optimistic. Jessie did promise to do better, and I think she really meant to, but that didn't last long. A week or so later, almost in tears, she said, 'I really like your class. It isn't that I don't want to come. Every day I plan to, but by the time that last hour comes, I just have to go home to sleep.'

"She came a few more times, but she couldn't keep up. Talk in the teachers' lunch room was that she failed all her classes that time around. And that eager look she'd had in September was certainly gone.

"The next year Jessie really made a good start, but it wasn't long before I heard that she was having problems getting to class and getting her work done.

"Winter trimester that year she was in my class again. It was a writing class, and one of the things we worked on was journals. Jessie's journals were revealing; she seemed quite willing to share her concerns. One of the things she couldn't understand was why she had so much trouble keeping up with school, although most of her friends seemed to get along all right. Another entry, though, indicated that she was unhappy because she didn't have as many friends as she thought she should. She felt pretty lonely, and, I'd guess, pretty inadequate as a person.

"There was enough evidence in the journals to make me feel that Jessie needed help, so I gave her name to the chemical dependency counselor. Pretty soon she came to class with a note saying that she'd miss our hour once a week so she could to go group. We worked out a plan for her to get her assignments done, and for a while she did fairly well. At least she passed that class.

"Several weeks later, Jessie's name turned up on the list of kids who were hospitalized. I asked her group leader about her, and she said that the group had felt that Jessie needed more help than they could give her. They'd confronted her with the evidence they had seen and she'd agreed. The school year ended while she was out, so I didn't see her again that year.

"Now Jessie's back in school, not in my class, but I see her a lot. She's got some good clear ideas about what she needs to do to graduate. From what I hear, she's carrying them out fairly well. She's got a pretty heavy load of classes, and she's working on a couple of correspondence courses from the U. She's just as pretty as ever, but the wide-eyed look is gone, of course. She still looks a little scared now and then, but usually she's pretty much in control. She'll make it."

"Speaking of making it," another teacher might enter into the conversation. "I saw that kid we used to worry about, remember? Joe what's-his-name. He's apparently doing quite well in the printing course at vo-tech, and he wants to go on to the University for a degree in some area of communication or graphic arts. He thinks he can get in there after he's proved he can handle school work. I really worried about him when he used to fall asleep in my first hour class. He just wasn't getting anywhere at all.

"He finally got far enough behind so that he agreed to come in for some extra help and we had a chance to visit a little. Apparently he decided I wasn't going to hassle him, because he arranged to come in once a week for a while. One day he came pretty late, after most of the department was empty, and he stayed around a little to talk. It turned out that the reason he was falling asleep so much was that he was working so many hours outside of school that he wasn't getting enough sleep anywhere.

"After we'd talked a few times, I asked him why he worked so many hours. It finally came out that he was really just trying to avoid being at home. Apparently his dad was a pretty heavy drinker, and when he was drunk he'd abuse Jim pretty badly. Not so much physically, I guess, because Jim was a pretty big kid, remember? But other kinds of abuse are just as bad. Jim had acquired a pretty low image of himself. His dad had always expected Jim to do pretty well in school. Apparently he'd tested pretty high as a child, but as things went along he didn't do too well. He just wasn't living up to his dad's expectations, and the farther he'd drop behind the worse his dad treated him. He finally got the job just to get out of the house.

"When I saw him last week, we had a cup of coffee together and Jim told me how much he'd learned from group here at school. One of his friends had talked Jim into going to group with him, and Jim said that that experience had made a lot of difference in his understanding of his family. He told me that up until he'd started at group he'd thought that everybody else's family was like families in TV commercials — happy and doing things together all the time. He'd been afraid that the reason his family didn't have those good times was really his fault.

"In fact, although he didn't say so, I got the feeling that he had even felt that his dad drank because Jim was such a disappointment to him. Getting out of the house was about all he could think of to do, but that wasn't working too well either. Anyway, Jim said that the kids in group showed him that he really had to take care of his own life. If he couldn't get his dad to some kind of treatment, at least he could be sure that he himself was not drawn into feeling responsible for the drinking. Jim made it through school, remember? He kind of picked up there near the end. Then when he graduated, he moved out on his own, got a job, and started at vo-tech. He thinks he'll make it now, and it certainly looks like he has a good chance."

One young man, Jeff Clem, is a good example of the success a concentrated program of treatment can have. Jeff talks easily about his experiences with chemical abuse and with freedom from abuse.

Jeff wasn't a likely candidate for dependency. One woman from the neighborhood in which he grew up says of him, "When he was in grade school, he was just the kind of boy any mother would like her own child to be." Jeff, however, describes his introduction to pot and booze.

"I started drinking early in junior high," he says. "When I was in seventh or eighth grade I went to a party where there was a lot of booze. Somebody had some pot, and the kids talked me into trying it. I liked it right away. I really got high in a hurry."

From those early junior high days, Jeff recalls that he used pot and booze quite regularly. When he moved on into tenth grade, however, he began trying other drugs. Speed, acid, cocaine, angel dust — he tried them all. Through it all he still used booze, and there was always pot.

Like many high school young people, Jeff rarely spent much time at home. "I'd be there at mealtime," he says.

"I'd say 'hello' and eat pretty fast and then I'd go out again." There weren't too many hassles with his folks, he remembers, except when he was high at home. He realizes now, though, that his parents were concerned and knew that he was harmfully involved. With the kind of knowledge that parents can acquire from a school program, the Clems took action. Jeff remembers the date when they decided that he really needed professional help.

"It was May 19, 1975," he recalls. "I'd come home pretty high and they just said, 'We've arranged a bed for you at St. Mary's. You're going into treatment.' I was so drunk I just said o.k. and went out to my car."

His parents were pretty determined, because they got into the car with him. "I drove myself to treatment," he says. "The folks must have been terrified. I was all over the road."

He got there, though, and began what he sees now as the most significant interval in his life. He's put the feeling into verse, which he calls "Treatment." He begins:

It's a big responsibility;
You can help yourself to grow,
And if you do not do that
You'll be putting on a show.

Looking back at that period in St. Mary's, Jeff recognizes that an individual really has to accept the responsibility for his own situation and for his own growth. Unless one does take a good look at himself, he is just playing a role. Jeff knows, however, that this is not always easy. Although inpatient treatment is structured and carefully planned — "There is yoga in the morning/And a group that starts at four" — not everyone is able to come face to face with himself. "If you will not face yourself/You'll be running out the door."

One of the things Jeff recalls from his period of abuse is the poor self-image that grows as abuse grows. Treatment emphasizes the positive points about an individual and tries to bring him out of the depression which often is part of the poor image.

It's a place to become aware of yourself
And the good things you can do.
But if you will not help yourself,
You always will be blue.

He has no desire to fool anyone, however. Even now when Jeff can look back at that period in the treatment center and can see its real value, he recalls its pain.

Treatment is very painful
For everyone I've known.
I've seen them cry, I've heard them yell
But I know they all have grown.

Through the pain of self-examination and the fight to be free of dependency, one of the valuable aids is the recognition that no individual has to be entirely alone. For many people a religious belief is a tremendous help, as almost everyone who becomes free of chemical abuse comes to recognize that no individual stands alone or is expected to do everything for himself. Jeff's verse comments on this:

There is a higher power,
You should relate to Him
Because if you don't do that,
Your life will be very dim.

But even with assistance from some kind of higher power, an individual must move slowly and must not expect to be successful all at once. Indeed, the verse says, "It comes bit by bit."

One of the unhappy things Jeff recalls from treatment is that not all people were successful in sticking through the pain. "A lot of people come/And some people go," he says. Here, he tells us, he means that those who go just split. In vernacular, of course, splitting is more than just going. Those who split really choose to be out of a whole experience. Those who stay mourn for them. "It really hurts to see/The stuff that they don't know" the verse states.

Jeff sees as a lifelong advantage the fact that treatment places vital emphasis on family and friends. "My parents, my sister, and my brother-in-law all went through treatment with me, even though they weren't chemically dependent. They got a lot out of it, too." Out of that common experience has grown a real closeness for the family, one which Jeff says they still share. That closeness has made him enthusiastic about the fact that anyone — dependent, harmfully involved, or straight — can profit from the self-examination, the self-understanding, the sharing, and the closeness which are part of the program. Again his verse underlines this thought:

> Treatment has its good points.
> There is a lot of caring.
> And if you will accept it,
> There will be a lot of sharing.

Like many others who have remained sober following treatment, Jeff feels that in a basic way, participation saved his life.

If you won't accept treatment
There is one thing you can do.
That is go and kill yourself.
There are lots of people like you.

In saving his life, treatment prepared the way for a successful future for Jeff. Since May 1975, he has not had a drink, nor has he used other forms of chemicals. He enjoys a close relationship with his parents and with his sponsor in A.A. He has a girl friend who supports his sobriety. That prospect of a successful future wasn't easily earned. Coming back to school, for instance, was an extremely difficult step. He found that for a period of time his old junkie friends remained his friends, but as he refused to get high with them, they drew back. Making new friends is not easy for a kid who has a reputation for heavy chemical abuse. This, of course, is where the value of a school support program becomes obvious. Jeff recognizes this. "I really lost a lot of so-called friends," he muses, "but I found a lot of real ones."

His verse ends

If you make it through treatment,
It can be the best thing in your life.
You'll come out a hell of a person
And you'll live a happy life!

So far his sober life has been a happy one for Jeff. He is positive about his future and what it holds for him, and he has moved ahead in a direction which indicates that those positive feelings have a firm foundation. He has his own apartment now, his own independence, and — more than that — his own business. He has formed a small company which contracts with builders and contractors to clean up

new houses, wash windows, freshen carpets, and generally prepare new homes for new owners. The company is
doing well. With the personality and good sense which
were part of the boy "that any mother would like her
child to be," and with the confidence and clear self-
understanding which developed through a stressful period
in his adolescence, Jeff can indeed look forward to a
happy life.

Chapter Eight

Enabling, Confrontation, Compassion

Only a hermit remote in some wilderness cabin can remain untouched by society's use of chemicals. Only the individual who can structure his life without regular human contact can avoid the effects of someone's abuse. Statistics show, for example, that an alarming number of drivers on streets and highways have had enough to drink to impair their judgment. Most people know fellow workers in offices, factories, or schools who regularly operate at low efficiency because of chemicals or who are frequently absent.

It is not at all unusual, in the course of one's daily activities, to encounter someone who shows the physical effects of chemical use, and, of course, use of chemicals is part of almost every social event. Even churches are relaxing their traditional attitude toward alcohol. Harmful involvement with chemicals seems to touch everyone, directly or indirectly. No one can say with confidence,

"This really doesn't affect me at all."

This is a circumstance which advocates of a chemical dependency program in the public schools will need to point out and illustrate. Figures relating to use and abuse are disturbing. The statement that 12 to 15% of the large number of our population who use chemicals will become dependent is certainly significant. One out of seven is a large proportion, a real cause for concern. However, that 12 to 15% may become addicted still leaves 85 to 88% who probably will not; one addict out of seven users leaves six who can continue to use responsibly.

It is typical of society's reaction to figures that most people quite optimistically see themselves on the more fortunate side of these statistics. Vital, therefore, in developing community programs dealing with harmful involvement is an emphasis on the role each individual plays in shaping and advancing the involvement which those around him suffer. It is essential to realize that it is almost impossible for an individual to become chemically dependent without support from those around him. Many of those people who feel so confident that chemical dependency will not affect them are in a very real way contributing to the dependency of another individual. At the very least, they are not helping another to overcome harmful involvement. In their bland assumption that they are not involved, many people become enablers.

In the language of harmful involvement with chemicals, the word "enable" has taken on special meaning. Most people use "enable" in a positive sense. Parents establish savings accounts which will *enable* their children to go to college; bus companies provide rate cuts which will *enable* senior citizens to get around economically. The definition has positive implications. *To enable* is to give strength or authority sufficient for the purpose.

All personal relationships involve enabling in one form or another. On the highest level, enabling may be very positive. Parents enable students to learn well in an atmosphere which encourages them; they can enable their children to develop the kind of independence which will serve them well in adulthood. Faculty members enable one another to perform at their best level, and administration enables both staff and students to move ahead. Teachers certainly enable students to grow academically and emotionally so that they can go on to school or work with confidence in themselves and in their abilities.

In the language of dependency, however, "to enable" has negative implications. Enabling is the aspect of the program in which the whole community participates, and this is the aspect which makes it impossible for anyone to say truly, "This really doesn't affect me at all." Those who make it possible for another individual to become harmfully involved with chemicals are said to be enabling him. They are enablers. Interesting, too, is the fact that in the language of dependency, the idiomatic use of the word is also modified. Although in its positive sense the word requires completion — someone enables another to do something — in its special use with dependency, the word is often used as a complete thought. A woman enables her husband in his dependency. A teacher who allows a student to shirk responsibility is enabling.

Enabling within the family follows some predictable patterns. A wife enables her husband if she makes excuses for him when chemical abuse interferes with job responsibility. Many wives will decide to avoid social events because of the problems which arise when husbands abuse. This is a form of enabling. A resourceful woman making an effort to keep her family functioning may become a kind of supermom, taking upon herself extra work and responsibility to smooth the way for her husband.

In her sincere and understandable effort to keep harmony within the household, she may exhaust herself, endanger the health of the family, and ease the way for her husband's further abuse. Sometimes, unable to cope with the frustrations of continued failures, she may rage at him. This also is a form of enabling.

In the delusion created by his abuse, her anger provides him with an excuse for continuing that abuse. "Who wouldn't drink," he now can say, "if he had to live with a mean-tempered shrew?" Caught up in her husband's disease, a wife may take all the responsibility for it upon herself, or she may meet the frustration of being unable to stop him from drinking by deciding to join him in his use. Either of these roles threatens her own emotional health and the emotional health of the whole family. It is easy to understand why chemical dependency is known as a family disease.

Husbands, of course, are not the only ones who abuse, and society is beginning to recognize the growing problem of the woman who abuses. In families where this is true, husbands become enablers and the pattern is only slightly altered.

In school situations, external forms of enabling may be different, but the basic effect remains the same. Some enabling smooths the way for the teacher who abuses. Since a larger number of people are involved in this relationship, enabling can go on for a long time before anyone is conscious of it. In order to keep things functioning smoothly in a school department, for example, several teachers may step in to accept responsibilities which really should be equally shared. Teachers who pride themselves on being more flexible will accept less desirable room assignments, because they know that one of their colleagues does not adapt to change. Somehow teaching assignments are adjusted so that one or another individual is not expected to teach during the first hour of the day or is not expected to develop a new course.

Several factors contribute to this kind of enabling. Many teachers are involved, so no one person sees what is happening. What is really best for the students is the deciding factor in most department decisions, so one teacher's reluctance to take on courses he or she doesn't like is often accepted. The desire to keep things functioning well is strong enough to justify many accommodations for an individual who is abusing.

Like the husband or wife who avoids social contacts because of a spouse who abuses, faculty members may eliminate activities involving similar contacts. The individual who is harmfully involved with chemicals may withdraw almost completely from any kind of social relationships within the faculty, or within the department of which he is a member. Others in the faculty or in the department see this withdrawal as a kind of rejection and cease to seek out their colleague. This kind of passive enabling allows an individual to become quite separate from the rest of the group. It allows that individual to believe that he or she can get along perfectly well without any give and take with other people; it allows him to retreat into the lonely world of abuse.

The husband or wife who gives in to anger has plenty of counterparts on school faculties. The faculty member who abuses often unconsciously invites that anger. Dramatic

flare-ups between staff members or icy accusations fur-
nish excellent excuses for one who abuses with chemicals.
"You'd drink too if you had a job like mine." Or "You'd
drink too if you had to work with a principal like mine!"
Or, perhaps, "You'd drink too if you had to deal with
these people I have to work with!" Such rationalizations
are yet another symptom.

Another facet of enabling within the school is, of
course, that which involves students. In the course of an
average school day, teachers work with a large number of
students. Recognizing the needs of individual young
people becomes increasingly difficult as the numbers grow
larger. Recognizing those needs, however, is a necessary
part of avoiding situations which enable young people to
abuse with chemicals.

This pattern in which teachers enable students is much
the same as those patterns involving family enabling the
student or the faculty enabling other faculty members.
The attempt to smooth the way is common. Often
teachers will simply lack the time and energy to deal with
an individual student in a difficult situation. If compromises seem necessary to keep class activity running
smoothly, a teacher may well be tempted to make those
compromises. If it simply becomes easier to relieve a
student of responsibilities, to provide him with materials
rather than to cope with the consequences of his failure to
provide his own, to coax him to do make-up work rather
than to go through the channels of dealing with parents
about absences, teachers may take the easier path. Allowing a student to ignore responsibility is, in a sense, to
encourage weakness and to discount the student's value as
an individual. To permit a student to by-pass his personal
responsibilities undermines his independence, in fact, it

implicitly encourages dependence, often dependence on chemicals.

Avoiding personal relationships of teacher with students is another kind of enabling. If young people find the relationship between teacher and student difficult to sustain and choose to withdraw, teachers are all too often willing to let them do so. If the withdrawal originates in insolence or in a cold shoulder to friendly approaches, teachers — who after all are people, too, — will often let the student retreat from such a relationship. This is understandable and there are many ways to rationalize it, but it is also, in many cases, a form of enabling which gives the student an excuse to fill his loneliness with chemical abuse.

Anger and the often-accompanying discipline administered in anger combine to form another type of enabling for which a teacher can be responsible. Education degrees do not bestow sainthood. Teachers lose patience, and they may very well erupt in anger. Certainly there are times when anger is completely appropriate. But a teacher's anger brought on, even invited by, a student who is abusing often ends up as a form of enabling. The anger itself becomes the issue and in the mind of the student the reason for it fades. Just as in the case of a family member or a faculty member, anger provides an excuse for abuse. "You'd drink too if you had a teacher like that!"

One of the most effective countermeasures to enabling is "confrontation." Here again the language of chemical dependency programs imparts a special meaning to a familiar word. For most people the word "confrontation" carries connotations of belligerency or of hostility.

In defining the word, some dictionaries recognize those feelings. The language of chemical dependency changes the connotations of "enable" from positive to negative. In this case the reverse is true. The language of chemical dependency emphasizes the positive qualities in the meaning of the word "confront." When one individual confronts another, in the special context of the Wayzata program and programs similar to it, one individual reveals to another his understanding of what is involved in the situation the two share. There should be no suggestion of belligerency or hostility.

On the contrary, in support groups, in relationships between two people of the staff, or in relationships between teacher and student, confrontation involves concerned sharing of what each individual sees as really happening. Ideally, of course, confrontation is calm and rational. In practice, naturally, it may not always be a calm experience.

However, the effectiveness of real confrontation depends upon a clear understanding of the effects of anger. Remembering that anger is frequently a form of enabling, that an individual who is abusing with chemicals can use anger as an excuse for further abuse, the person who confronts another tries to keep cool. Effective confrontation exposes facts, states reasons, and shares concern. In every possible way, effective confrontation recognizes and counteracts enabling.

One of the major difficulties in any program, of course, is the fact that it is considerably easier to point out what not to do than it is to recommend what should be done. It is reasonably easy, once one has given some thought to it, to identify behavior which is enabling. It is also reasonably easy to recommend confrontation and to point out that confrontation must be reasonable, calm, and marked with concern. It's quite another thing to act according to this advice.

As they grew up in our society, most adults shared experiences which taught the values of cooperating, sharing, lending a helping hand, or trying to ease the burdens of another. Caring for one another often takes the form of helping one another in concrete ways. Parents express their love for their children by doing things for them. Smoothing the way for someone who is growing up can't really be wrong, can it? How can caring people learn to distinguish between expressing concern and enabling?

These are the questions which each person must ponder for himself. Each person involved in a program dealing with harmful involvement with chemicals has to find for himself some measure by which he can determine the difference between caring and enabling. Perhaps the measure lies in exercising genuine compassion and empathy, in making a genuine effort to feel with another person.

What an individual sees as he looks out on his or her world every day is a picture which is uniquely his own. Each person's experiences shape and frame what he sees, and since no two people share the same experiences, no two people see the same world. Because no one can see another person's world, each person tends to believe that everyone lives much as he does.

Those who live in a middle-class neighborhood, own two cars, a small boat or canoe, and a cabin at the lake carelessly assume that everyone lives in pretty much the same kind of neighborhood, owns cars of about the same vintage, enjoys a boat ride now and then, and spends weekends at the lake. Although they read about life-styles different from their own, most people really believe that others are just like they are — with the possible exception of presidents, kings, and queens — and consequently believe that everyone else is subjected to about the same pressures and shares the same desires.

If the people an individual knows share a six-pack of beer now and then and enjoy a glass of wine with Thanksgiving and Christmas dinners, he assumes that that is what everyone else does. If the people he knows get really drunk now and then, have an occasional knock-down fight with a spouse, and suffer real differences with their children, he thinks that is what life is all about.

A good program in a school district, a really good program which attempts to deal with more than symptoms of harmful involvement with chemicals, will have to begin with this human characteristic in mind. Everyone sees life differently, but everyone believes that others see life as he does. And too often, although he honestly knows better, he tends to believe that everyone would be better off if all people would only act as he does.

One goal of a good school program should be to develop the awareness that people do see life differently. Each picture of the world is unique, but each has value. One person's way of life is neither inferior nor superior to another's. Each person must separate this awareness from any kind of judgment or evaluation. What each person shares with another is what he feels or what he sees. He may say to a friend, "I see you moving away from the group and I miss your contribution to it." He may say, "I see you missing school days much more often than you have in other years." He does not say, "You shouldn't miss so much school" or "You're leaving too soon after school's out. You ought to stay around longer." People learn to share feelings, to share what they see, but they learn not to make judgments.

So a good school program will develop compassion, a feeling for one another. If people can indeed feel their friends' pressures, problems and desires, they will not judge. They can only share concerns and fears, and hope that in that sharing they can introduce new dimensions which allow their friends to make their own evaluations. This is what good confrontation can do, if that confrontation grows out of true compassion.

No program is going to be able to develop compassion in all members of the school community in one school year. It probably is not going to develop that feeling in most people even over a period of several years. A good program, however, can begin. It can begin to show people that not being involved is a form of enabling; that good confrontation is not judging, but rather sharing one's view of what is happening; and that real compassion benefits everyone. Everyone can grow when others begin to care.

Chapter Nine

Some Negative Reactions

It would be pleasant to report that success for the Wayzata School District Chemical Dependency Program came swift and sweet. In many ways it did. Encouraging signs from the beginning kept its organizers moving. Certainly the number of students who found help from counselors and groups was impressive, and stories of individuals who began to move away from abuse were satisfying. To suggest, however, that every step was successful and that good feeling always prevailed would be wrong. Anyone who begins such a program will have to be prepared for many negative reactions. Success comes slowly; sometimes the mood is distinctly sour.

Negative reactions to the program will occur. A basic problem with these negative reactions will be to determine whether they arise from those who are threatened by and afraid of the program because of their own use. Recognizing the fear allows people working in the program to accept this angry kind of opposition. Once this kind of acceptance occurs, dealing with the problem of abuse becomes the major issue, as it should. The barrier of anger can then be handled appropriately.

Negative experiences with the program fall into two categories. On one hand are the one-time difficulties, difficulties which arise with any new and somewhat controversial program. Leadership will shift and parts of the program will have to be re-shaped to fit the shift. New teachers and students will have to be educated and some old teachers and students will have to be re-educated about the goals of the program. Mechanical problems of scheduling and demands for building space will have to be met. These are, fortunately, one-time problems. Even though they may represent real challenges for a time, they can be faced, handled, and overcome.

On the other hand is a second kind of negative reaction, more elusive and more difficult to handle. Those who plan to begin a program dealing with harmful involvement with chemicals should anticipate some continuing reactions which cannot be met head-on, handled, and settled once and for all. Interestingly enough, these problems will often manifest themselves through problems with language.

One kind of negative reaction concerned with language revolves around the distaste some people feel about jargon, about a pattern of language which belongs to a particular group. In-service programs, training groups, counselors, and eventually organizers of programs have their own special language. Expressions such as "That's where I'm coming from" or "I'm o.k. with that" quickly enter the daily speech of participants and set them apart. It is in the setting apart, apparently, that trouble lies.

Advocates of a program will want to be careful that an elitist feeling does not develop.

Any form of elitism or feeling of belonging to a special group can cause problems within a school. This is particularly true in the case of harmful involvement with chemicals. Many members of a community, in spite of all education to the contrary, will continue to feel that the problem of abuse with chemicals is a moral one. These people particularly may resent any suggestions of elitism among those working in any way with harmful involvement, even when that work is aimed at providing a way out of the pattern of abuse.

Resentment becomes more severe if cost is a factor and other favorite programs must be cut back. Moreover, an elite or special group implies that there are also outsiders. No one wants to be an outsider, even if what one is outside of is a group whose uniting force is pain and unhappiness.

Those who work with a school program will have to recognize and understand the attitude of those who react negatively. Complaints about language will often mask these feelings of resentment or alienation, and those who are working in the program may be inclined to dismiss those complaints as ridiculous. Simply dismissing — or, worse, scoffing at — objections to jargon will only aggravate negative reactions. A clear-eyed look at the basis of objections, an honest evaluation of whether there is an elite group forming, and an acceptance of the possibility that individuals may feel alienated will ease the way.

Another facet of the language of dependency programs is the question of profanity. The emphasis on open expression of feelings which is part of the philosophy of treatment often results in language which polite society deplores. Wayzata has had ample evidence of that.

"I got tired of kicking kids' asses out of school." The lead paragraph of a front page article in the *Minneapolis Star* for March 3, 1976, quoted Dr. Manning's response to a question about how Wayzata's program had begun. Reactions from the community — in this case the larger community of the *Star's* readership — were not altogether positive. Dr. Manning received a number of letters.

Mr. Principal:
Watch what you eat or drink. I might put something in your food that will not allow you to speak like you do.

This letter, of course, was not signed, but another was.

Sir:
In your position of principal is it necessary for you to use such low-brow language to express yourself? Such remarks as "kick his ass out," "damn awful way," "get the SOB out of my classroom." This only points out that you have lowered your standards of speech to that of the offenders.

Then the choice of D. Anderson as an advisor was a real master piece. His vocabulary runs pretty much to such remarks as "pissed off," "bullshit," and I'd guess he has others just as obscene.

Isn't your job one of supervising a teaching staff? These little darlings didn't acquire their rotten habits while in school. Send them home to their parents and let them straighten them out. It's not your problem as "Principal" of a school.
                    Respectfully,

Others were no less abusive, and just as negative.

Dear Dr. Manning:
I wish to express my disgust and disapproval of the filthy language attributed to you and Don Anderson in the March 3 article in the *Minneapolis Star*. Such profanities and attitudes are ill-befitting the dignity formerly expected of, and exhibited

by, educators of American youth.

Clean up your foul mouths, both of you, and be a decent example to the students and the tax-payers in this area.

Yours truly,

Mr. Manning —
THE ABUSIVE LANGUAGE USED BY YOU IN THIS ARTICLE CERTAINLY MAKES YOU A ROTTEN EXAMPLE FOR OUR YOUNG FOLKS.

DIDN'T YOU EVER LEARN TO MASTER THE ENGLISH LANGUAGE AS A STUDENT — OR, DID YOUR PEERS SPEAK AS YOU DO???????????

AN IRATE MOM

Letters to the editor of the *Star* voiced the same opinion:

To The Editor:
What a sorry commentary on the public school system when a man in an administrative position must resort to verbal garbage to express his ideas!

Surely more sophisticated minds than mine must voice their rebellion and consider it an affront to our sense of decency that you published as a lead article the one about Wayzata High School students who get help with their drug and alcohol problems (March 3), couched in such vulgar language as was attributed to their principal.

In my opinion, it is more than the students who seem to need help in that school.

Minneapolis

To The Editor:
Granted profane frankness might be a part of getting at personal weaknesses and self-deceit in group therapy sessions. But a professional with any degree of competency must have a better basic vocabulary, one that the students and teachers he works with would do well to emulate.

St. Paul

This is only a sampling of the responses to the article. A careful reader of these letters, however, will have real difficulty determining what the subject matter of the article actually had been. Anyone who had missed the March 3 issue of the *Star* would find in these letters only one hint as to the real issue. Only one refers to "help with their drug and alcohol problem."

Completely aside from his or her reaction to the language of the article, the thoughtful individual cannot help but be dismayed by the attitude revealed in those letters. That attitude is clearly indicative of what those who organize a program dealing with harmful involvement with chemicals must face. These writers missed the point entirely. They failed to observe that beneath the language they deplored was a message of hope for many young people. They allowed themselves to be preoccupied with superficial concerns to the point that they ignored the really significant ideas.

Anyone beginning a program of action against harmful involvement with chemicals will be frustrated by encountering some preoccupations with superficial matters. An excessive concern with language was one such preoccupation and it may be defensive, of course. It is entirely possible that a preoccupation with language is a mask for fear, because any program requiring in-depth self-examination represents a threat. Ironically, preoccupation with superficialities is typical of the roots of many youngsters' harmful involvement with chemicals. Young people traditionally distrust anything which is phony or which places more value on appearances than on real feelings. Young people often choose language for its shock value, for its ability to move straight through politeness to real feelings.

Sometimes language which is carelessly chosen obscures ideas rather than communicates. When the question of language becomes the major issue, other issues remain hidden. The whole question of language choice, then, carries beneath it fundamental questions young people feel within themselves as part of the insecurity which leads to abuse with chemicals. Is society only concerned with superficial qualities, with appearance and cover-ups? Are real feelings o.k.? If I let my real feelings show, will I be giving too much of myself away?

One of the major functions of support groups is to encourage individuals to be honest with themselves and with others. Cover-ups, superficial niceties, and all forms of pretense cloud feelings and suggest that those feelings are somehow unworthy. Unless restraint in language arises out of a recognition of the rights and feelings of others and a concern for others, that restraint is dishonest.

Although a program that emphasizes respect for oneself and an accompanying respect for others can recommend restraint if unrestrained language is clearly offensive to one's listeners, among groups of people who genuinely understand one another and who have genuine mutual respect, choice of language becomes unimportant. No individual requires others to speak as he does, but everyone respects everyone else's right to make his own choice.

However, there is a lesson to be learned from the community reactions to language which general opinion regards as foul or profane. One of the continuing problems a school program will face is the problem of community support. Those most closely involved with public relations must be sensitive to community feeling, and it is not politic to defy public opinion in an area as easy to control as choice of words. No group will respond well to requests for assistance and support if those requests are phrased in ways which are offensive to members of the group. And anyone asking respect for his ideas in working out a program must respect the ideas of his listeners.

It is significant that positive responses to the articles in the *Minneapolis Star*, responses which indicated that readers genuinely understood the program and respected its goals, outnumbered negative responses eleven to one.

Success will come. Small successes will have to suffice for a time, and negative reactions can be handled. They will, however, be handled most effectively if people who are most concerned will recognize and deal with the real problems on which negative reactions are based rather than with what those reactions appear to be.

"When Will We Be Through?"

"When will we be through with this program?"

Someone always asks the question. Particularly when budget matters must be discussed and when, as is more and more often the case, a school district is forced to decide where to cut expenditures, the question will be debated. Those who support the program will need to fight every year for their allotment of district funds.

One of the satisfying experiences people have is the experience of recognizing a problem, tackling it, and solving it. Few things are more frustrating than recognizing a problem, expecting to solve it, and having to tackle it again and again. In the case of harmful involvement with chemicals, the only way to avoid this frustration is to recognize that chemical abuse may be a problem which does not have an easy, at-hand solution. Concerned people have to accept the fact that this particular problem must be addressed again and again and again. A school district may never be through with it, just as it is never through with new students.

The only permanent solution to the problem is prevention. The simplest definition of prevention, of course, is "to keep from happening." The question, "When will we be through with the program?" really means, "When will we be able to keep abuse of chemicals from happening?"

Prevention of use seems almost impossible and is not truly desirable. Our society takes the use of alcohol for granted. If individuals invite friends in for a nightcap, they don't mean for hot chocolate. Everyone understands that. Ask a group of people how many of them had not had a drink between 3:00 a.m. and 8:00 a.m. on any given day and they will probably all raise their hands. "Drink" for most people doesn't mean coffee, tea, or milk, and certainly it doesn't mean orange juice. Society simply assumes that the words "a drink" mean alcohol in some form. And when a cocktail lounge advertises its 5:00 to 7:00 o'clock late afternoon service as the "attitude adjustment hour," it is clear that contemporary society assumes that chemicals will have mood-altering effects.

Movies and television support this assumption. Characters turn to a drink as a reward at the end of exhausting action, or they radiate sophistication at a cocktail party. In many movies, being drunk is funny, not unpleasant or dangerous. Even cartoons for young children use intoxication as a source of humor. Obviously the use of alcohol is accepted and a large number of people use alcohol responsibly without abuse. We know, however, that abuse among teenagers is increasing.

Thirteen- to fifteen-year-old youngsters are now using regularly. Attracted by the notion that alcohol is a reward for effort, that it is a sign of sophistication, or that it will help to adjust an attitude, these young people find that getting high is pleasant. It makes them feel relaxed, one of the crowd. Too often, though, the pleasantness of getting high progresses to the pain of abuse. And parents are faced with the question, "Could I have prevented my youngsters' using?"

As a parent and also as part of his experience with harmful involvement among high school students, Dr. Manning has given a lot of thought to that question, and he shares his reflections with other parents.

"Could I," he asks himself," have kept my own youngsters from using? If I had not used, would my youngsters not have used? We know, of course, that the greater share of youngsters who use come from families who are users. I certainly presented my youngsters a role model that would encourage their use. I never beat my wife or ran out on her. My youngsters saw me high, but never physically abusive when high. I taught them that chemicals can be used for relaxation, that problems fade when we use. When we use chemicals, we don't have to be up front with our feelings; those feelings can be buried.

My youngest is a senior in high school. If I had my preference, none of my four children would use anything. I know, however, that this is impossible. I know that teenagers and young adults today like to get high. It's difficult to convince them that an occasional high on chemicals is not necessary. Moreover, it's difficult to convince them not to use when their peers use. It's difficult for them to be active socially and not use chemicals. In most instances the chemical is alcohol, alone or with pot. On the addiction scale, I believe, alcohol is more dangerous than pot."

Dr. Manning admits to fears, fears which are familiar

to many parents. "I still am afraid," he says, "when youngsters anticipate a weekend and look forward to getting high on chemicals. When getting high is the main goal of the weekend, when getting high brings about the camaradarie that they like with their peers, then I'm afraid. I'm afraid of the anticipation and of the need to get high with chemicals. Then I begin to reflect. I remember those same anticipations for those same reasons. Yet now I find it impossible to ever look at getting high on chemicals."

These fears, however, have led Dr. Manning to an examination of his own use. He explains. "Two years ago I made a commitment. I would never again use chemicals to get high. I regret having to be fifty-one years old before I made this decision. One of the reasons that I feel so deeply and devoutly that this program is necessary is that I now realize we must begin as parents and as educators to teach children how to get high without chemicals. Some adults hate the word *high*, but getting high is a unique experience. How we get there is vitally important.

"As I look at the word *prevention*, I have to recall what has happened in my life and the changes that have occured since this program began at Wayzata High School. The most visible change to those who know me is that I don't abuse alcohol anymore. I don't drink and get high. It's an obvious change, a change that's good for me physiologically. It's a change that my friends recognize. It has cost me some moments of togetherness with some of my friends, I'm sure, but of itself it really doesn't mean anything more than that I have opted not to abuse alcohol. I am not and was not chemically dependent, although I believe I could have become so. The decision that I will never again get high on chemicals wasn't difficult for me to make. The most difficult thing was to make the decision that when and if I take a drink, it has to be under different circumstances than it was before.

"Being a leader in the school program has brought less visible changes. I have tried to change in my dealings with other people. I hope that I have changed in my dealings with my own children, that I treat them differently than I did in the past. That kind of change is not, perhaps, visible to other people. The change is on the other side of a narrow line, beginning in my recognition of things that were buried deep inside me. I'm opinionated and aggressive. I believe I've always been that way, though I'm not sure why.

"Those characteristics I don't believe I've changed. I *am* opinionated. I *am* aggressive. A couple of years ago I would not have admitted that. But just the recognition of this narrow line that separates two distinct ways of behaving has helped me, I think, to deal better with other people. Knowing that I tend to be opinionated and aggressive, I realize how others probably see me. As a result, I understand their reactions better. I have found growth and peace through my willingness to share my thoughts with others and this sharing has helped me sort out feelings that have been hidden for years.

"It was difficult for me even to admit to having feelings. Perhaps it was the macho instinct that kept me from saying that I had tender feelings and that I felt strongly about things. I *did* care. I *was* concerned. I also had anger hidden under strict and straight outward appearances. I believed that emotions and feelings were personal and should be kept to oneself, and I believed that other people were not interested in how I felt. I believed that it was unmanly to cry, and that belief goes back a long way.

"A most significant episode occured when my grandfather died. I was eleven years old when my dad wakened
me one morning and said he had something to tell me.
Before he would tell me, however, he made me promise
that I wouldn't cry. When I had promised, he told me that
my grandfather had died. I didn't cry. I wanted to, but I
didn't. I've since looked at my dad's reasons. He certainly
was not an unfeeling person. I believe now that he didn't
want me to cry because he felt that if I cried, he also
would, and that, he believed, would have been unmanly.

"So, as I was raised by two fine parents, I developed the
unconscious feeling that it wasn't right to cry when one
felt pain. I don't recall a time when I did cry, but I believe
now that the greatest disservice a man or a woman can do
their sons is to tell them that it's unmanly to cry.

"I grew up with other feelings. Some said that it was
wrong to touch. These feelings suggested that touching
had a sexual connotation, a need for a sexual act. When
our program at Wayzata began, one of our high school
counselors told me that one thing he was sure would
happen to me personally and to us as a group was that
people from the Johnson Institute would teach us to hug.
To think of hugging a male was repulsive to me. This
feeling had kept me from hugging my own sons when they
became teenagers. This feeling went back a long way to a
time when I felt that a display of affection to one of the
same sex was perverted. I had, I think, always felt that
intimacy and sex were always connected. Now I know
that intimacy can be a gentle friendly touch, a hug, or just
the words telling close friends how much I think of them.

"I recall a brief incident while I was attending the
Johnson Institute's training session. A nice woman in the
group had decided that nowhere in her life was there need

for intimacy. She had two children, but her reason for having children had been to carry on the family name. She indicated that she and her husband did not have sex any longer. She was not any longer interested in touching anyone or in having her husband touch her, not even to put his arms around her. She had built up such a resistance to him that she had programmed herself into believing that even in living with another person there was no need for intimacy.

"She was in the group because her husband was chemically dependent. With the skilled leadership of the Johnson people, this woman, through many hours of counseling, came to recognize her needs and to know that the reason she was so adamantly opposed to touching was her reaction to her husband's use and abuse of alcohol. Out of his use and abuse had come a family illness. The family had disintegrated to nothing more than four people living in the same house.

"Not recognizing my needs had kept me partially unfeeling for almost fifty years. Masking feelings in chemicals, denying inner thoughts, desires, and feelings by abuse of alcohol, and being unwilling to share my thoughts and feelings with others had kept me from feeling — openly feeling — and had kept me using. Recently I had a period of a few days during which self-imposed job pressures kept me out of touch with my true feelings. I felt lonely, lonely because of my unwillingness to share with people whom I trusted. When I did recognize the fact that I was stuffing my feelings, I was able at least to bring them out in front and deal with them appropriately.

"Why all this self-confession? Why? Because I believe that this is where we must begin with our children. I do not believe that prevention should begin with present high school students. I believe that the best thing we can do with the high school student is point out over and over the progression of dependency. I believe we must try to teach students the value of feelings. We must help them appreciate and understand their need for intimacy. And we need to help them see the dangers of ignoring or suppressing their feelings.

"High school students today can't visualize themselves as chemically dependent. To them the terms "chemically dependent" and even more certainly "alcoholic" describe the fallen-down drunk. In our school we have quit making diagnoses and trying to determine whether a student is chemically dependent. We do know that when pain results from chemical use, there is a problem, or there is the beginning of a problem. That is why we speak of "harmful involvement." If an individual is involved with chemicals at any time and nothing negative occurs from that involvement, obviously there is not yet a problem.

"Any time pain comes from use, however, there is harmful involvement. Early recognition of harmful involvement is what we watch for and what we emphasize as important for both students and faculty. For that reason, programs at junior and senior high schools must do more than discuss factual information about alcohol, narcotics, and tobacco. They must look at something deeper than use; they must look at feelings, needs, self-concepts. We must quit waiting for the secondary student to become dependent before we become concerned. We need to begin to see whether negative results are coming from use. Together with students we must look at feelings, we must recognize our needs, and we must lead the way to dealing with feelings and needs, without depending on mood-altering chemicals.

"Where will prevention come from? When should we begin to try it? How do we do it? These are questions for which none of us has sure, indisputable answers. We can only take stock of what we have done so far in our program and of what we feel are some of the positive things we are continuing to do.

"I do not feel that it is possible at this time to put down a list — one, two, three, four — the things that must be done to prevent abuse. But we have learned some things. The first is that it is probably o.k. to use alcohol. We are living in a society that approves of alcohol use. It is important that as parents and teachers we begin to accept responsible use. We must decide that it is all right to use as long as use is responsible, without harmful involvement, without pain. For years, clergymen preached from the pulpit, parents preached from home, and numerous organizations preached in public the need for abstinence, prohibition. The preaching attempted to find a legal way to put a stop to use. But we haven't found any stopping. We haven't found that preaching led to prevention. Some people, of course, still believe it is not right to use. No one can criticize or contest this belief.

"It is right to say, however, that one person's belief that using chemicals is wrong will not guarantee that other people will agree. That is obvious when we think of the number of people who use in the United States. Neither preaching nor legislation are effective in counteracting abuse, nor do they work particularly well in guaranteeing appropriate use. For this reason, I think, it is vitally important that we take the mystery out of use. Appropriate use should be presented to our youth not as an ideal, but as a norm that is useful and pleasureable. As adults

and teachers, we should present role models of appropriate use, if we are going to use. We must never present the
idea that problems can be solved or that problems need
not be faced if one uses.

"Along with being a family disease, alcoholism and
addiction is a "feelings disease." People who are abusing
and who are dependent are not only physically addicted;
they are also emotionally addicted. The chemical is
helping them through hard times. It is not allowing them
to openly and directly take a good hard look at their
feelings.

"In my opinion, prevention of abuse, if prevention is
going to occur, must begin at a very young age. It should
begin even prior to school, but we in the public school
systems have the opportunity to provide experiences that
will aid prevention. Public school systems must make an
honest attempt at the early elementary level to teach both
parents and students how to deal effectively and honestly
with their feelings. We must teach positive self-concepts,
positive feelings about ourselves. We must teach young
children to recognize feelings, not to bury them.

"Using again the example of a first grader who has a
dog which dies, we can look at the school's role. We can
teach that first grader that it is normal and acceptable to
be sad and to cry over the death of the dog. We should
not minimize the hurt in this child's heart, nor should we
ignore it. Grieving is a healthy part of living. It is vital for
parents to recognize the grief, the hurt, and the loneliness
in their child's loss. They must encourage the youngster to
recognize that he or she is hurting because the dog is dead.
This is, of course, over-simplification. It is, however, an
example of an opportunity for parents to become
involved with their youngsters. How many times have we

heard parents say to a youngster who has fallen down, "Don't cry! Be a man!" or "Don't cry, dear, it's only a dog." That is wrong, and it is not helpful. It is important to encourage a child to recognize and to express feelings.

"We in the schools must also try to teach children alternative highs. How does one get high without the use of a chemical? We might teach children to look at each day and find something good. We might teach children to say, "Gee, it's a beautiful day!" We might teach children to talk out their problems, "Gosh, I feel awful today. My mother and father had a fight last night, and I was scared."

"We must teach parents to include in their family life ways to experience highs without chemicals. Skiing down a slope is certainly a high. Listening to music can certainly be a high. Many youngsters use pot while listening to music because they feel that they can hear more — that they can hear better when they do. As parents we have to try to teach our youngsters that music in itself can produce highs if we listen carefully. We must try to teach our youngsters through our own example that physical activities like running and manual labor can produce highs. And in school districts we must constantly promote self-esteem and positive self-concept groups."

So, what then can be done?

There is not any totally right way to work for prevention. Self-respect and self-concept groups will not do it alone. Education courses pointing out the pitfalls of abuse will not do it alone. Just getting youngsters and adults into treatment will not do it alone. Teaching youngsters alternative highs will not do it. And making it o.k. for people not to use will not do it. We must teach the fact that chemical abuse is a disease that affects millions of people. We must teach the fact that a combination of all the above may only begin a program moving in a positive direction.

It is vitally important to repeat here that no program will succeed until its leaders are willing to look at their own use. The greatest single factor, the most important thing that has happened in the total Wayzata School District Program is that someone in a position of authority in the Wayzata Senior High School has taken a look at his use. The second most important fact is that someone in a position of authority in the Wayzata Senior High School has recognized that there are many feelings and factors that have influenced his life and that only through constant evaluation of himself and where he is going will he continue to feel good and to present a role model that is positive in promoting the program in the Wayzata School District.

Once we recognize these values in the program and identify the kinds of actions we can take to achieve those values, we may have to answer the question, "When will we be through with the program?"

Maybe we'll never be through. The most we can hope is that working with elementary level youngsters we eventually will develop teenagers who can use chemicals in a responsible manner, if they use at all. Eventually, perhaps, a number of young adults will have positive self-concepts which will make it possible for them to avoid abuse. And when that happens, perhaps a new generation of elementary pupils will need less instruction in how to handle feelings. Perhaps they will have better options than turning to chemicals. Perhaps, just perhaps, some future generation may even be able to say, "We're through."

Chapter Eleven

New Thoughts and Feelings

When will we be through? That's been a question ever since the program at Wayzata began. Now, three years after the first publication of this book, the question seems almost naive. We probably never will be through. More realistic questions which program participants should ask are these: What are we doing to prevent drug use? Can we see some changes as a result of the program at Wayzata? What's happening across the country? Are there some things that we didn't see three or four years ago that show promise in this program? Answers to these questions are more hopeful — hopeful enough to encourage Dr. Manning to make a career change.

"In June of 1981," he explains, "I left Wayzata High School to devote the rest of my professional life to the field of chemical dependency. That decision to leave was not because I was dissatisfied with the school. I felt good about the school system and about the things that were happening there. Most certainly the students at Wayzata

High School are some of the finest in the United States. The faculty is also of the highest caliber. I don't believe that any principal could have had a more cooperative group than I had at Wayzata. I decided to leave, however, when I realized that I was receiving so much from this program by sharing it with other parts of the country and that sharing took priority. I will also be honest and say that I hoped for and needed some free time myself. That free time was simply not available to me while I was principal.

"Since this book was finished in 1978, I have had some changes in my own attitude concerning alcoholism, just as I have seen some earlier ideas confirmed. One change relates to reactions to treatment. As people across the nation begin to share programs and ideas concerning both adolescent and family use of chemicals, interventions and treatment have become less traumatic. The thought of going into treatment is much less threatening and the thought of doing an intervention on loved ones is regarded as loving concern, not as a violation of rights. As more people exhibit a fairly contented sobriety, other people are more willing to say, "I am an alcoholic" or "I was addicted to a drug." More and more members of our communities are apparently willing to look at their own use and, perhaps, to adjust that use by going through treatment, by attending A.A. meetings, or by just changing their lifestyles. This lack of trauma is very encouraging. Intervention and treatment weren't easy for these people. The experiences aren't pleasant to begin or even pleasant to complete. However, as young people return from treatment and find support in the student groups, parental support groups, and A.A., both teenagers and adults are less threatened by the prospect of entering treatment.

"Another change in my attitude is really a change in focus. Treatment and intervention have not lost their importance; new programs, however, emphasize earlier prevention and seek to help children develop valuable life skills. Two school districts in Minnesota, along with several others across the nation, have introduced programs which reach all levels — kindergarten through twelfth grade — to deal with problem-solving techniques and the development of feelings of self-worth and self-esteem. Without necessarily discussing the use of chemicals, these programs focus on prevention. During the past few years I have come to believe that focus on this kind of program is vital.

"Project CHarlie — CHarlie is an acronym for Chemical Abuse Resolution Lies in Education — was the first program of this kind. It began in Edina, Minnesota, when a group of Edina residents contracted with their school district to introduce a program that would allow consultants to enter each classroom once a week and share with the teacher and class methods to help children deal with their feelings, make proper decisions, and develop feelings of self-worth and self-esteem. Project Pride — Pride is an acronym for People Relate in Desirable Environment — followed CHarlie in the Wayzata School District. The only difference between the two is that, while the Edina program uses outside consultants who come in and replace the teacher, the Wayzata program uses teachers presently in the classroom. Both projects have the same goals; both work to establish self-esteem and self-worth; both teach proper problem-solving techniques, responsible decision-making, and the establishment of positive peer relations.

"As similar programs occur across the United States, they are meeting with success. These programs confirm my earlier beliefs that prevention of abuse must begin early. They also provide opportunities for implementing those beliefs."

School districts with programs of this nature establish priorities and indicate to their teaching staffs that a portion of each week is to be set aside for specially designed activities to accomplish goals like those of Project Pride and Project CHarlie. Teachers learn to recognize youngsters with problems. They try to establish one-to-one relationships with youngsters who are hurting. In addition, teachers learn to introduce into their academic programs organized lesson plans that help a child learn to spell feeling words or learn to seek out ways of making proper decisions. Plans allow the entire class to express their feelings. Such programs involve hours of organization, writing, and planning. They also require inservice training of the teaching staff. Moreover, parenting classes involve parents who wish to become part of the program.

Along with this, teacher education attempts to point out ways teachers' own attitudes can affect students in their classes. As good as our educational system is, it still includes many teachers who do not realize that they must be aware of and interested in their students as unique people. These teachers must be continually educated in techniques for dealing with individuals. Administrators must give teachers responsibility in their classrooms and those administrators must show confidence in the teachers' work. Teachers must know that they can arrange their time to deal with students individually; they do not always have to give top priority to accomplishing a certain amount of work in each class. Private and personal communication with students must have a very high priority rating. Most of all, teachers must serve as role models for students and, at the same time, demand excellence and competence from them. However, these demands must be accompanied by guidance toward achievement.

At a recent national convention, one of the speakers listed four different areas in which a teacher might question his or her own effectiveness:

The first area is *freedom and challenges.* Teachers should ask themselves these things: Do I encourage students to try something new, to join in new activities, to have a voice in planning the classroom and a voice in making the rules they follow?

A second area is *respect and warmth.* Do I learn the name of each student as soon as possible? Do I share my feelings with my students? Do I arrange some time when I can talk quietly with each student?

Classroom control is the third area. Do I remember to see small disciplinary problems as understandable and not as personal insults? Within my limits, is there room for students to be active and natural?

The final area is *student success.* Do I permit my students some opportunity to make mistakes without penalty? Do I make positive general comments on written work? Do I give extra support and encouragement to slower students? Ideas implied by these questions are very simple and yet vital to the establishment of feelings of self-worth and self-esteem.

Project CHarlie was one of the first to recognize and
define factors present in most people who are abusing
chemicals. It is difficult to determine whether these factors
contribute to chemical dependency or whether they are
characteristics already present in individuals who become
dependent. In any case, however, six factors deserve
careful consideration.

Factor Number One — Lack of Drug Awareness

It is clear that though people may be involved with
alcohol and drugs, many lack full knowledge about some
consequences of use. Teaching about drug awareness is
not adequate. Educators have spent a great deal of time
developing health courses designed to prevent drug abuse
at the junior and senior high school levels. Most of these
health courses have centered on factual information about
drugs and about how those drugs affect us physiologically. More education is necessary, not only for teenagers
but also for adults. That education must concentrate on
the many, many effects of chemical abuse. School health
programs and adult education programs must change
their direction in teaching. Factual material is not enough.

We need to teach people why alcoholism is a disease.
We need to teach them that alcoholism is primary,
describable, progressive and permanent. We need to
emphasize that alcoholism is fatal. Along with this kind of
teaching, we need especially to deal with our young
people and some misconceptions in their thinking. These
misconceptions are widespread. Everyone has heard some
young person say, "I'm too young to be an alcoholic," "I
only drink and smoke pot occasionally," "I can quit any
time I want," or "I never drink on weekdays, only on

Saturdays." These are all familiar expressions. They are also all examples of misguided thinking.

It is necessary to teach our youth how this disease progresses through four stages to dependency. These four phases were identified by Dr. Vernon Johnson, author of *I'll Quit Tomorrow.* Teaching people about the four stages will at least give some insight into the insidious way dependency progresses through Phase I, the learning stage; Phase II, the seeking or planning stage; Phase III, the harmful dependency stage; and Phase IV, the chronic or fatal stage.

It is also necessary to teach the way a family is affected by chemical dependency. Sharon Wegscheider, in *Another Chance, Hope and Health for the Alcoholic Family,* examines the way a family responds to chemical abuse. Such a family rapidly becomes dysfunctional. Instead of the drawing-together experienced by a family facing the terminal illness of one of its members, the family suffering from dependency experiences separation. This breakdown of the family was described in an earlier chapter of this book, also. Experience confirms these observations.

People must also be taught the stages of recovery. The child in the alcoholic family needs to know that just because the father has been through treatment, things will not be all right again immediately. Both the child and the family must understand the very important phases of recovery — denial, compliance, defiance, acceptance, and, finally, surrender. Understanding these stages places the family members of the dependent in a better position to accept the fact that recovery is a long-term process. It just doesn't happen as a parent, a sibling or a friend leaves treatment.

Drug awareness teaching must also contain information about the physiological dysfunctions that occur with heavy use. People also need information about pharmacology. They must remember that if a drug puts them to sleep, calms them down, reduces their pain or anxiety, or stimulates them in any way, that drug is extremely dangerous.

Factor Number Two — Stress

Most people experience stress. None of us has been lucky enough to get by without feeling stress and the suffering which results from not being able to deal with it properly. Stress is sometimes confused with a popular term that many people use today when they feel overworked or locked-in. Today's popular term is burn-out. Burn-out is, for some, a legitimate term synonymous with stress. It can, however, be used as a cop-out. Current discussions of burn-out can support people who feel locked-in, unable to find options to an undesirable position. The notion of burn-out can really create a paralysis of indecision. Paralyzed and indecisive, people who feel burned-out are not only unwilling but unable to prioritize the demands in their lives. Sometimes burn-out is just an extension of an over-extended ego, an ego that says, "Yes, but if I don't finish this now, my job will be at stake," or "Yes, but I can't prioritize these tasks because they are all important." That famous "Yes, but" allows these people to stay within their problems. This is not burn-out; this is stress.

Stress exists and can be handled. Just recognizing a stressful position is a healthy step toward reducing some anxieties and pressures. Crucial to this whole business of chemical dependency, however, is the need to recognize that people use chemicals to eliminate stress. They have a very tough day with a problem; they find that a couple of cocktails relaxes them and takes the stress away. As adults we teach our children that a pre-meal cocktail really deals with the stress of the day. It is interesting that adolescents use marijuana about the same way adults use alcohol. Drug awareness teaching must include a discussion of marijuana. When teenagers are willing to share their ideas about drug use, they may say, "Look, I've had a bad day. A joint mellows out the problems; in fact, a joint does away with the problems." With this lack of drug information and inability to deal with stress, the student gets into difficulty. We are beginning to learn some very simple things about marijuana and its chemical ingredient, THC — Tetrahydrocannabinal. When THC is ingested, it has two effects. One is residual. No organ in the body detoxifies THC, as the liver detoxifies alcohol. THC is attracted to the fatty cellular tissue of the body. Ingested through the smoke of marijuana, it enters the blood stream and goes to the fatty cells of one of the fattiest organs we have in the body, the brain. Researchers believe that the body takes about seventy-two hours to rid itself of the THC contained in one marijuana cigarette. A student who continues to use marijuana every day will have a constant supply of THC in fatty cellular tissues. The insidious thing about this is that, as students begin to use marijuana, they do find that it mellows out the problems of the day and relieves what youngsters think is stress.

However, marijuana does not relieve stress. It relieves the symptoms of stress. Just as a physician might medicate a patient to relieve severe head pains without relieving the reason for the pain, the student self-medicates with a marijuana cigarette assuming that because the marijuana does away with feelings of anxiety and stress, it also does away with the problem. Students believe that this is the way to deal with stressful situations, when in reality it is just a way to eliminate *symptoms* of stress — bury stressful feelings and forget the stressful situation. They are not working on the cause of the stress itself.

Because researchers are beginning to find evidence of stress in almost every chemically dependent individual, we need to teach both students and adults how to recognize stress and how to deal with its cause. We need to teach people to differentiate between symptoms and causes.

Factor Number Three — Poor Problem-solving Skills and Lack of Ability to Make Responsible Decisions

From the problem of stress we move to the third factor usually present in chemically dependent people, an inability to make responsible decisions and the lack of problem-solving techniques. As problems surface, stress settles in. Without the ability to solve problems, individuals find themselves locked into stressful situations. They may resort to chemicals. Problem-solving ability certainly isn't inherited; we need to *learn* how to solve problems. Schools must help children develop skills in this area. Schools could also make a major contribution by giving parents an opportunity to learn proper problem-solving techniques. Business and industries work to help employees acquire these skills. Unfortunately, however, not enough groups are looking at this need.

An incident last year in school illustrates a student's inability to solve his problems. Herb walked into my office one day, abruptly announcing that he had been kicked out of a class. Role-playing the situation with him, I discovered that he had gone late to class. When the teacher asked him why, Herb answered that he had had to go to the bathroom.

"Why didn't you come to ask permission?" the teacher asked.

Herb's retort was, "If you'd had to go as badly as I did, you wouldn't have asked permission."

When the teacher asked Herb to take his seat, he didn't. In the argument which followed, the teacher asked Herb to stay after school; Herb, however, made an obscene gesture and walked out of the room.

When Herb reached my office, his complaint was that he had been thrown out of the teacher's class. After our look at what had actually happened, I reacted to the first problem. That problem was gross insolence. Herb's gesture and his walking out of class were unquestionably insolent. The school has a punishment for that and Herb understood why he was being punished. He accepted that result, because he knew he had made an obscene gesture.

The situation could have ended there, but I knew that the next part of the problem was a little bigger. I asked Herb, "What's the problem?" He was quick with answers. "I had to go to the bathroom." "I walked out of the class." "I was late to class." "I made an obscene gesture." I pursued the question. "What's the problem?" Ultimately, Herb unwittingly found the answer when he blurted out, "I don't know what you're talking about, but I hate that teacher's guts!"

Clearly Herb had found the problem. Walking into that class, Herb had not recognized or been willing to recognize the fact that he really disliked the teacher. Instead, he had set that teacher up by being late to class, by using the excuse of having to go to the bathroom, by not taking his seat when asked, and finally by making an obscene gesture. He had zinged the teacher, discounted him in front of the class, and then made an arbitrary decision to leave the class. When I asked Herb, "Would you do that to me?" he said, "No!" Then we sat down and tried to see the real problem, his dislike of that teacher.

We had identified the core of the matter. Now the search for a solution could be appropriate to the real situation. We were no longer avoiding the issue by punishing behavior that was only a symptom of a problem which could grow worse until it was identified.

Lee M. Silverstein, in his book, *Consider the Alternative*, talks about problem-solving. He sees this skill as nothing more than techniques and devices that allow us to have some choices and then to choose the most appropriate choice. Silverstein suggests that first we brainstorm all possible solutions to a problem. Then we place those possible solutions in five categories — most likely, most desirable, most probable, most possible, and most undesirable. Once we've been able to classify all our imaginative ideas, we can decide which solution is most possible. Many times that solution will not be the most desirable. It may, indeed, take a very painful direction. Certainly we are not always able to come up with a solution which is both desirable and easy. We can, however, teach children how to use problem-solving techniques which will lead to responsible decisions.

Looking at responsible decision-making, I find that I have changed my philosophy since this book was first published. I said then, "I think it is vitally important that we take the mystery out of the use of chemicals. Appropriate use should be presented to our youth, not as an ideal but as a norm that is useful and pleasurable. As adults and teachers we should present role models of appropriate use, if we are going to use." This is not bad in itself. What has become more important to me now is teaching people how to make responsible decisions about use. In advocating appropriate use of chemicals, I advocated appropriate use. This approach, however, doesn't take into account those who do not want to use at all. I have changed this philosophy over the past year. I now feel that what we have to do is teach people to make responsible decisions about every area of their work, their personal lives, as well as their chemical use.

Responsible decisions are not made by shooting from the hip. They are not made as a result of stress. Responsible decisions are made when all possible solutions are identified and we are able to view various solutions and their probable effects. With this real change in attitude, I feel a vital aid toward eliminating chemical abuse is good problem-solving techniques and the ability to make responsible decisions.

Factor Number Four — Curiosity and Boredom

I am not sure whether these are contributing factors in chemical abuse or factors just naturally present in young people, but adults recognize both curiosity and boredom in their teenagers. Adults honor curiosity in children. We want them to be curious about math, science, and good literature. We want them to be curious enough to take risks, to join the cast of the musical at school or to try out for the class play. We want them to be curious enough to want to take an advanced language course, to learn to play a musical instrument, to throw a piece of clay on a potter's wheel, or to take part in interscholastic or intramural athletic activities. All of the things that we want our kids to be curious about are positive.

On the other hand, we do not want our children to be curious about sexuality, about homosexuality, or about different religions. We do not want our children to be curious about different political systems. Of course, some parents are not threatened by their children's learning in these areas, but many parents absolutely refuse to allow their children to be curious about anything that they have not accepted.

We also are not too fond of our children being curious about alcohol and drugs. We quickly forget that many of us have provided our children with role-models that make alcohol, at least, attractive. Most of the times we have used alcohol have been socially acceptable. If use becomes a problem, so that the family has become dysfunctional, the child is still unable to see chemicals as the cause. As adults we have placed chemicals in an acceptable category. Yet some of us would not want our children to be curious about what we find so attractive in chemicals. Accepting the fact that it is healthy for children to be curious about many things is a step in the right direction.

I recall a parent's coming to see me quite upset because she had discovered her child reading a popular magazine which she regarded as pornographic. She was afraid that her child would become a pervert because of the magazine. None of us wants children to read sex-oriented magazines. Certainly a child who dedicates a great deal of time to reading pornography should be guided in other directions. However, sexual curiosity is a natural characteristic of healthy young men and women. Accepting this curiosity allows parents to deal with it appropriately, without implying that the child is dirty or wrong.

Along with curiosity, parents must recognize boredom. Not long ago a mother described to me how her son went to school at 7:40 in the morning, was busy with school until 2:10, practiced football until 5:00, and then worked at one of the local grocery stores until 9:00. He reached home about 9:30, watched television until 11:00, went to bed, and got up each morning saying that he was bored. Her honest concern was "How can my son be bored when he is so busy?" I explained to that mother that probably the first step to finding an answer was for her to accept the fact that apparently her son was getting no strokes at all in his busy sixteen-hour days. Little in school seemed to be giving him what he wanted. He apparently didn't really enjoy football. He had begun to work to buy a car. Once he had the car, he worked only to maintain it, so the thrill of owning it was over. When he came home in the evening the family had very little to do together.

When the mother asked me what I thought should be done, I didn't have a solution. The thing I thought we ought to do first was discuss with the boy whether he really wanted to go out for athletics and then find out what his real interests were. We discovered that he really was interested in construction work. The school helped him change his schedule, recommending that the next term he attend a vocational school for part of the day, entering the building trades unit. He took his required English and Social Studies classes one hour before school in the morning and during the first hour of the day. Between times, he attended vocational school. Less than three months later his mother described an entire attitude change.

Vocational school isn't always the answer, of course, but the fact is that each of us needs to have something about the day that we enjoy. If we enjoy a portion of every day, we do not get locked in with boredom and stress. Curiosity and boredom may not be contributing factors to chemical abuse, but they certainly are factors to recognize as part of a natural growth period in adolescence.

Factor Number Five — Lack of Healthy Peer Relationships

There is not any question about peer pressure. It exists from early childhood until the later years of life as a normal experience. The acceptance of peer pressure is a step toward dealing with it. Many experts believe that students experience a tremendous amount of peer pressure directed toward the positive side of their activities, but some is also directed negatively. We know that in a sick and dysfunctional family, peer pressure is particularly strong. Youngsters give their lives to their peer group. They make extra effort not only to belong but also to conform. They reject family teachings in favor of the values of their peers. Their need to be accepted by the group is far greater than any family pressure.

Many parents object to their children's friends. One instance occurred last year. A mother new to our community expressed her pleasure about moving into a school district that had committed itself to Pride, where vandalism was very low, and where problems in chemical abuse were being addressed. She was very happy to be here and hoped that her son would now be rid of the "junky" friends he had had in a southern city. She expressed her hope that her son would establish new relationships.

My statement to her then would be the same today. "Unless something drastic occurs, your son will have the same type of relationships here that he had in your home town." To help her understand, I asked her to describe the friends they had had in the town they had left. They had belonged to a country club. The friends they had there had been very good friends. Coming to Wayzata, the couple had joined the country club and had established some relationships very similar to those they had had in the old home town. These new friends were the kind of people they enjoyed being with, people who liked to play golf, bridge, and tennis, who enjoyed good meals and good times. I pointed out to her that probably her son had the same kinds of relationships with friends in this home town. His friends were not acceptable, of course, to either her or her husband, but that did not mean that her son had not enjoyed a relationship with a group of young people to whom he related happily. Just as she and her husband had gravitated toward people like their old friends, so her son would naturally find friends like those he had enjoyed. What could she do? She and her husband would have to give conscious effort to creating change. Her son's natural gravitation toward a familiar group had to be arrested.

About three and a half years ago, I experienced peer pressure. One evening my wife and I were invited to a party with a group of friends. On the way to the party, my wife said she wanted to drink Tab with a twist of lime. At the party we guests mixed our own drinks, so I fixed her Tab and lime. I filled my glass with ice cubes, poured charged water over them, and added a splash of Coca-Cola. I stirred it up and walked into the group, comfortably secure. What I didn't realize then was that I had manufactured a drink that looked like either scotch or bourbon and soda and that was what had made me comfortable. It dawned on me several months later that I had felt tremendous pressure to be like the group. I didn't want to give my friends any reason to believe that I was different. My wife, of course, was very content with her Tab and lime. She, apparently, did not feel the pressure I did to appear to have an alcoholic beverage in my hand. I suffered from peer pressure as great as any child suffers. Although I did everything in my power not to drink, I still was not self-assured enough to say, "Hey, I don't want a drink tonight."

On the other side of the coin, lack of healthy peer relationships is something entirely different. We encourage children to have friends and then, when they choose their friends, we pass judgment on their choice. When they don't bring their friends home, we automatically conclude that they have something to hide. It is very possible that their friends do not fit the mold that we want for them, and so they feel uncomfortable introducing those friends to us. Families must change that routine. We must find ways to give our youngsters alternate and solid experiences in developing healthy peer relationships. This experience, moreover, must include specific discussion of how to develop relationships without the use of a chemical.

The Wayzata School District has attempted to do this in several ways. Many years ago our music department offered opportunities for all youngsters to learn to play the piano or the guitar. Later, courses were added in advanced piano and guitar. This was an opportunity for our youngsters to learn a leisure-time activity. It was also an experience that placed a youngster with a group of others all of whom were enjoying a healthy activity. School people hoped that this would carry over into their private lives. There is no guarantee that a simple program like this will prevent chemical abuse, but there certainly is no reason to discount the idea that perhaps we might be teaching alternative ways of getting high.

The school has also provided a course in Outdoor Education. Students do everything from cross-country skiing and camping to canoeing and rock-climbing — all activities designed to create alternative highs. The course has been very well accepted. A large number of youngsters who have gone through chemical dependency treatment have opted one of these programs.

Programs will not, of course, prevent abuse. It is important, however, to remember that programs like this might contribute to prevention by providing natural highs, by providing opportunities to establish healthy group relationships without the use of chemicals. Quite a number of our students at Wayzata High School during the 1980-81 school year got together to organize a chemically-free dance, and a variety of other activities they chose to be chemically-free. Before my last graduation as principal, I asked the senior class of almost six hundred to treat their graduation night with dignity. I asked all of them if they would at least try not to drink alcohol before the graduation exercises. Perhaps because it was my last graduation, or perhaps because there was a lot of emotion involved, I may have overlooked someone who had been drinking, but as the students came across the stage I was very, very proud of them. I am not naive enough to believe that there had been no drinking. Certainly, however, there was none that was obvious.

Adolescents do find rewards in not using chemicals, especially when we can establish groups of them who have that goal.

Factor Number Six — Self-esteem and Self-worth

If there is one factor that's missing in every chemically dependent person I've met, it's a feeling of self-worth. If every adult and every child could wake up each day feeling good about himself or herself, we would have taken a giant step in teaching people how to live their lives. If we could look to the good things every day, perhaps there would be no need to use chemicals. We may be able to teach people alternative ways to get high, but in order to do this we must strengthen self-esteem.

How does one go about establishing self-esteem? We all know that we don't just wake up with that good feeling some morning. Self-esteem is a growing, learning part of our lives, and it takes years to develop, or to destroy. There are lots of easy answers to the question of how to develop self-esteem. Boards of education and the public may insist that we begin to develop feelings of self-worth; they may believe that a winning team, a new look in clothing, a change in the color of the rooms, or a change in staff will effect a change in degrees of self-esteem. There must, however, be a sounder basis for emotional health, both in children and in adults. Whatever we expect ourselves to be is what other people expect us to be.

If I feel good about myself, I will be caring with other people, but I will also recognize that I am the most important person in the world in relationship to my own health. This is truly the beginning of a positive self-image. The idea applies also to children. The way children feel about themselves is the way they are going to live. Somewhere I read that self-esteem is based on a child's belief that she is lovable and worthwhile and that she matters just because she exists. Arnold Lazarus says in his book *I Can If I Want It*, "High self-esteem is not conceit. It is a child's quiet comfort about being who he is."

The way I react to children affects their self-esteem. In order to deal with a child on a positive basis, I must present a positive attitude. If I respond negatively, the child is going to fail. When I mirror the student as being very adequate, very good, I give enough personal positive feelings to that person to create energy to attack some of the problems to be met that day.

When I allow children to make mistakes, I also allow them their dignity. By allowing them to be wrong, I recognize that they have a right to change. They are not mature individuals. Without an opportunity for different daily experiences, they are not going to fail, but they are also not going to succeed. Our children have a right not only to success, but also to failure. They need to learn how to correct mistakes.

The first step to high self-esteem in children is having parents or teachers who feel good about themselves. When adults feel good about themselves, they can be empathetic to youngsters. With empathy, we do not need to judge. Only when adults are in touch with their own true feelings can they give a child the total support that child needs. Teachers can, of course, be good teachers without establishing a goal of developed self-esteem in their classrooms. Teachers can, however, be excellent teachers if they have this development as one of their goals. Becoming role models of people who have their act together should be a major goal for those who want to promote high self-esteem among children. Getting at the problem early is important.

There is no absolute guarantee that recognizing these six factors will help prevent chemical abuse among teenagers or adults. The credibility of the Pride Program, however, can rest on occasional small incidents which reflect its influence. One such incident occurred in May, 1981. In a conversation with one of our senior high school parents, who also had an elementary student, I learned that the man had really not been sold on the Pride Program until just that spring. His business one day was just not going well, so he decided to leave the office and go home in the early afternoon. He was sitting on the back patio when his younger son walked in, went to the kitchen for something to eat and came back to the patio. Looking his father over, he said, "Dad, you look sad today."

The father told me that he was tempted to deny that sadness and smooth it over by saying, "Oh, no big problems, I just came home early." He had, however, attended a parent meeting where Pride was discussed. He recognized a great opportunity to talk with his son about being sad. Instead of minimizing his feelings or glossing them over, he said, "You know, I really am kind of sad today, and kind of down. I had a bad time at the office and I just decided I'd come home and try to work it out."

Telling me about this, he said, "I asked my son if he knew how I felt. We had a marvelous conversation about how it was for him to feel sad and how it was for me to feel sad, but most important, we agreed that it was all right for both of us to be sad at times."

This father was convinced that Project Pride was responsible for drawing his child's attention to the word, sadness, and for encouraging the boy to risk confronting his father on those feelings. This is a truly healthy family relationship.

Parents can do many things to encourage communication of this type. I like to suggest that families around the supper table try to report something good that happened to them that day. If we begin to program families into looking for something good each day, to expecting that something good did happen every day, we can focus on the high points of our experiences rather than on the lows. It's also a good experience, however, for families to express some bad things that happened that day. It has got to be okay to have occasional bad days. Feelings of jealousy, sorrow, loneliness, sadness and anger shouldn't be denied. We often teach children that these feelings are private and should be settled within oneself, not shared with others. What we forget is how much we discount family and friends by not sharing with them.

There are also times when we have to go out of our way to say nice things to people. An excellent goal for each and every one of us is to take time out every day to say something pleasant to someone to whom we haven't spoken pleasantly before. Making this a personal daily goal gives us a positive outlook. One of my goals in my last year as principal was to communicate in some positive way with two boys and two girls on each working day of the year. Sometimes I would make some positive remarks to students about their dress, about what they did in school, or about how I saw them progressing. Each communication had to be very positive. Some days the message might be just appropriately touching a student as I walked in the halls. Dealing with all young people, we should remember the value of touch.

When students are angry, it is very easy to be turned around and to use anger against them. It is terribly easy to get pulled into anger. It is extremely difficult to reach out and say, "You're really angry and it really hurts me to see you angry. I know you feel lousy about it, but I want you to know that I'm not angry with you." This approach is most certainly a good way of dealing with children. Just walking out and putting an arm around a student's shoulders sometimes renews a relationship. Sometimes this is the only way to say to a child, "I care for you."

The addition of this chapter to this edition has given me a great deal of comfort. The chemical dependency program at Wayzata High School, Project Pride, and the number of students these programs have helped are also a source of comfort and pride. I relish the idea that I do not have to overdose again. I thrive on the idea that I can now be sociable without feeling the pressure of having to take a drink or pretend that I'm taking a drink. I feel great satisfaction in being able to deal with people on a feeling level, to take the risk of saying, "I love you."

My involvement in this problem and the programs that have resulted from the problem have been very beneficial to me. No person has profited more, personally and emotionally. I challenge the readers of this book to become involved in chemical dependency programs. Dependency is a very insidious and a very frightening thing. Not becoming involved in fighting it lets the problem grow. Becoming involved is one of the healthiest things that can happen to us and to our families. Becoming involved means, first of all, TAKING A LOOK AT YOUR OWN USE AND AT YOUR OWN LIFE.